100 THINGS GIANTS FANS
SHOULD KNOW & DO
BEFORE THEY DIE

Bill Chastain

TRIUMPH
BOOKS

Library of Congress Cataloging-in-Publication Data
Chastain, Bill.
    100 things Giants fans should know & do before they die / Bill Chastain.
        p. cm.
    ISBN 978-1-60078-556-6
    1. New York Giants (Baseball team)—History. 2. New York Giants (Baseball team)—Miscellanea. I. Title. II. Title: One hundred things Giant fans should know and do before they die.
    GV875.N42C49 2011
    796.357′640979461—dc22

                                                        2010044067

This book is available in quantity at special discounts for your group or organization. For further information, contact:

Triumph Books
542 South Dearborn Street
Suite 750
Chicago, Illinois 60605
(312) 939-3330
Fax (312) 663-3557
www.triumphbooks.com

Printed in U.S.A.
ISBN: 978-1-60078-556-6
Design by Patricia Frey
Editorial and page production by Prologue Publishing Services, LLC
All photos courtesy of Getty Images unless otherwise specified

For Giants fans everywhere

Contents

1 Willie Mays

To the media and baseball fans alike, he was "the Say Hey Kid." Close friends knew him as "Buck." No matter what nickname Willie Mays went by, most remember him as the best all-around player to ever play the game of baseball.

Mays hailed from Westfield, Alabama, and learned how to play the game as a youngster by watching his father play in Industrial League games. By the time Mays was in high school in 1947, he had already begun to play professionally, first with the Chattanooga Choo-Choos then the Birmingham Black Barons of the Negro American League. The New York Giants signed him to a contract in 1950, and on May 25, 1951, he played in his first major league game, thereby beginning a memorable Hall of Fame career.

Mays' first major league hit was a home run off Boston Braves left-hander Warren Spahn. The hit came after Mays had failed to register a hit in his first 12 major league at-bats, prompting Spahn to joke about that encounter on many occasions during the years that followed: "I'll never forgive myself. We might have gotten rid of Willie forever if I'd only struck him out." Mays finished the 1951 season with a .274 batting average, 68 RBIs, and 20 home runs, which, coupled with his athleticism, were enough to earn him Rookie of the Year honors.

That first season would be a teaser for Giants fans since Mays got drafted by the Army in 1952 and missed most of that season before missing the entire 1953 campaign. That lost time in the major leagues cost him almost 270 games. Ironically, while in the service Mays did little else beside play baseball for the U.S. Army.

Willie Mays follows through on his swing while collecting a base hit against the hated Brooklyn Dodgers at Ebbets Field during a game in 1955.

He rejoined the Giants in 1954, establishing himself as one of the best players in the game. Not only did Mays lead the National League with a .345 batting average, he also hit 41 home runs to win his first Most Valuable Player award while also leading the Giants to the World Series, where they swept the Indians. During the Series, Mays made "the Catch," the name given to the over-the-shoulder grab he made on a drive hit by Cleveland's Vic Wertz in Game 1 (see No. 9, "The Catch").

In 1956 Mays became only the second player in major league history to hit more than 30 home runs and steal more than 30 bases in a season, with 36 home runs and 40 stolen bases. The Gold Glove award came into being in 1957, and Mays made the award his to keep, winning the award for the first 12 years after its inception.

Mays guided the Giants to the National League pennant in 1962 by leading the team in eight offensive categories, while also leading the majors in home runs (49) and total bases (382). A Mays home run broke up one of the more memorable pitching duels in major league history on July 2, 1963. Juan Marichal was pitching for the Giants and Spahn for the Braves, when Mays homered in the bottom of the 16th off Spahn for a 1–0 Giants win. That home run helped Mays earn the distinction as being the only player in major league history to hit a home run in every inning from the first through 16th.

After hitting 52 home runs in 1965, Mays won a second MVP award. He appeared in 24 All-Star Games during his career. Baseball immortal Ted Williams once said, "They invented the All-Star Game for Willie Mays." Mays finished his career with 660 home runs, which ranked third in major league history when he retired after the 1973 season, having spent his final two years in the major leagues with the New York Mets.

Mays went into the Baseball Hall of Fame in 1979. During the induction ceremony, he was asked whom he considered the best player he saw during his career, to which he answered, "I don't mean to be bashful, but I was."

The Say Hey Kid was just being honest.

2 Christy Mathewson

Talk about a lopsided trade, even Frank Robinson for Milt Pappas doesn't hold a candle to this one: the Giants traded right-hander Amos Rusie to the Cincinnati Reds for, gulp, Christy Mathewson. No doubt that trade, which took place on December 15, 1900, ranks as the best trade in Giants history and perhaps one of the top five trades in major league history. Though he would later be inducted into the Hall of Fame, Rusie got injured in 1901 and pitched in just three games for the Reds in what would be his final season (the beginning of an unfortunate pattern for the Reds). Mathewson, meanwhile, went on to win 373 games in 17 seasons, with 372 of those wins coming while wearing a Giants uniform.

Mathewson hailed from Factoryville, Pennsylvania, where he played sports as a youngster before attending Bucknell University. In addition to playing on the school's football and baseball teams, Mathewson served as class president. During his college years, he also played minor league baseball for some of the surrounding towns and earned All-America honors in football as a drop-kicker.

Mathewson elected to leave college in 1899 to pitch for Taunton of the New England League before moving to Norfolk of the Virginia–North Carolina League in 1900. He pitched so well for Norfolk that the Giants took notice and signed him. But after he went 0–3, the Giants sent him back to Norfolk and even asked for a return of the $1,500 they had spent to purchase him. Once Mathewson returned to Norfolk, the Reds picked him up, which set up the trade back to the Giants that took place later that year.

In 1901, Mathewson's first full season in the major leagues, he posted a 20–17 record with a 2.41 ERA. Two years later, he came

Christy Mathewson warms up in front of a big crowd before a game at the Polo Grounds in 1907. One of the greatest pitchers in major league history, Mathewson is tied with Grover Cleveland Alexander for third place in career wins with 373, to go along with an overall ERA of 2.13.

into his own with the first of four 30-win seasons. He complemented his 30–13 mark with a 2.26 ERA, and from 1903 to 1905 Mathewson won 94 games.

Mathewson anchored a Giants' pitching staff that played the Philadelphia Athletics in the 1905 World Series, pitching three complete-game shutouts in six days as the Giants won the Series four games to one. With Mathewson serving as the team's ace, the Giants won three additional National League pennants, but 1905 proved to be his only World Series victory. Mathewson's best season came in 1908 when he went 37–11 with a 1.43 ERA. He also had 34 complete games.

Frankie Frisch

Future Hall of Famer Frankie Frisch had his beginning with the New York Giants in 1919 when the "Fordham Flash" left Fordham University to sign with the team. He went straight to the Polo Grounds without ever playing in the minor leagues.

In Frisch's rookie season of 1919, he played in 54 games, hitting .226 with two home runs and 24 RBIs. In his first full season in 1920, Frisch showed marked improvement when he hit .280 with four home runs and 77 RBIs. In addition, he stole 34 bases. Frisch dazzled Giants manager John McGraw to the point where the hard-to-please manager made him the team captain while playing him at second and third base.

Frisch actually was McGraw's perfect player since he could handle the bat, understood how to play small ball, was a good fielder, an accomplished base runner, and had a high baseball IQ. While Frisch played for the Giants, they won National League pennants for four straight seasons and converted two of those pennants into world championships by capturing two straight World Series in 1921 and 1922.

Though a favorite of McGraw, Frisch had a falling out with the Giants manager late in the 1926 season when he missed a sign. In the aftermath of that blowup, Frisch left the team and was traded to the St. Louis Cardinals for enigmatic star Rogers Hornsby. Hornsby had some success for the Giants, but letting Frisch get away would be one of the worst trades in Giants history.

With the Cardinals, Frisch played in four more World Series, serving as one of the main cogs in the Cardinals' "Gashouse Gang" teams. He would play 11 seasons in St. Louis and capture the Most Valuable Player award in 1931 after hitting .311 with 4 home runs and 82 RBIs. Frisch played 19 seasons in all, with a lifetime average of .316, 105 home runs, and 1,244 RBIs. He was inducted into the Baseball Hall of Fame in 1947.

In July 1916 Mathewson was traded back to the Reds, who once again got a raw deal, as Christy pitched just one game before retiring as a player, though he did stay on to manage the team through the 1918 season. In Mathewson's 17 seasons as a pitcher, he started 552 games and threw 435 complete games. Complementing his 373 career victories were 2,507 strikeouts, a career ERA of 2.13, and an incredible 0.97 ERA in four World Series appearances (11 games).

Mathewson did his patriotic duty in 1918 by enlisting in the Army to fight in World War I. Earning the rank of captain, Mathewson served in the chemical service, which led to his being gassed accidently. That accident festered and later turned into tuberculosis. Once he returned from the war, he joined the Giants as a coach from 1919 to 1920, but his physical condition prevented him from being totally devoted to the team. He missed prolonged periods away from the team dealing with his illness.

Mathewson died in Saranac Lake, New York, on October 7, 1925, which coincided with the first day of that year's World Series between the Pittsburgh Pirates and the Washington Senators. Both teams wore black armbands throughout the Series. In 1936 Mathewson was elected into the inaugural class of the National Baseball Hall of Fame. He was the only one of the five inductees to be inducted posthumously.

3 John McGraw

John McGraw brought what had made him a good major league player to his job as manager, and the results were predictable: he became one of the best managers in major league history.

As a player, McGraw clawed and scratched and did anything within his power to win a baseball game. Some of his tactics as a player might have been considered cheating. For example, if a ball was hit in the air, he might take advantage of the umpiring situation that prevailed in his era, in which just one umpire watched the game. While the umpire watched to see if the ball was caught, McGraw might trip a runner or stand in his way. On the base paths, he might cut the corner rounding third, taking a route several feet in front of the bag to score more easily from second base.

While some considered said acts cheating, others insisted McGraw was simply employing gamesmanship. And nobody questioned the results, which generally saw McGraw on the winning side of the ledger. McGraw played 16 seasons in what was known as the major leagues prior to the 20th century. During that stretch of years that spanned from 1891 to 1906, McGraw hit .334, drew more than 100 walks in three different seasons, and had a .466 career on-base percentage, which ranks third all-time, behind Ted Williams and Babe Ruth.

The native of Truxton, New York, was a master of "little ball," or employing the little things into his team's day-to-day game plan, such as bunting, hitting behind the runner, and stealing bases. Home runs were simply not a part of baseball during the era in which he played, but they came into fashion during his later years as a manager.

McGraw's first year as a manager came in 1899 as a player/manager for the Baltimore Orioles, then of the National League, and he led the team to a fourth-place finish at 86–62. McGraw also managed the Orioles in 1901 and 1902, after the Orioles moved to the American League.

At the age of 29, he moved to the New York Giants in the second half of the 1902 season. He continued to be a player/manager through 1906, but played little once he took over the Giants. McGraw would remain the Giants manager until 1932, when he retired at age 59. In 31 seasons with the Giants, McGraw's teams went 2,583–1,790. Overall, he compiled 2,763 managerial wins, and his 2,669 National League wins still rank first, though his overall wins are second behind Connie Mack. From 1921 to 1924, McGraw led the Giants to four first-place finishes, making him the only National League manager to claim four straight pennants. With McGraw at the helm, the Giants won 10 National League pennants, three World Series, and finished second 11 times.

Back-to-Back Championships

Building on their 1921 World Series win over the New York Yankees, the Giants showed they were the class of the National League in 1922 when they cruised to the pennant by a seven-game margin. As in the '21 Series, the Yankees were once again the Giants' opponent, and the Polo Grounds would host all of the World Series games, since the Yankees also called the Polo Grounds home in 1922.

Joe Bush took the mound for the Yankees in Game 1 and kept the Giants off the scoreboard through seven innings. Trailing 2–0 heading into the eighth inning, Irish Meusel had a two-run single, and Ross Youngs added a sacrifice fly to lead a 3–2 Giants win.

Meusel accounted for all of the Giants' runs in Game 2 when he smashed a three-run homer off of Bob Shawkey in the first inning. The Yankees managed to tie the game at 3, sending the contest into extra innings. Both teams were stunned when umpire George Hildebrand ended up calling the game due to darkness after 10 innings, even though approximately half an hour of daylight remained.

Jack Scott, who had made an impact for the Giants' fortunes in 1922 when he posted an 8–2 mark in 17 games, continued his excellence by tossing a four-hitter in Game 3 as the Giants moved to a 2–0 lead in the World Series. With John McGraw at the helm, the Giants looked comfortable playing close games, which they reaffirmed in Games 4 and 5 when they took wins of 4–3 and 5–3 to earn the distinction of sweeping the best-of-seven World Series in five games— don't forget the tie.

Critical to the Giants' success was their pitching staff's handling of Babe Ruth, who had no hits in nine trips to the plate in the final three games. While the Giants appeared to be in the midst of their heyday, the 1922 world championship turned out to be McGraw's last.

McGraw became a part owner of the Giants in 1919, which allowed him to add the titles of vice president and general manager to his managerial duties, resulting in his having total control over baseball operations. Prior to his final season as manager in 1932, McGraw opted to retire his uniform and managed his last games wearing a suit and tie, before retiring completely midway through the season. In 1937 he was inducted into the National Baseball Hall of Fame.

4 Barry Bonds

Talk about a quality free agent signing. Take a look at what Barry Bonds did for the Giants after joining the team through free agency prior to the 1993 season. In 15 seasons wearing a Giants uniform, Bonds hit .312 with 586 home runs and 1,440 RBIs. He would become a seven-time National League Most Valuable Player, winning the award five times with the Giants—including four consecutive years from 2001 through 2004—and become baseball's single-season home run king as well as the all-time home run leader.

From the time Bonds was a young man growing up the son of former Giants star outfielder Bobby Bonds, he was earmarked for greatness, becoming a high school All-American baseball player at Junipero Serra High School in San Mateo, California, where he also played football and basketball. Upon graduating from high school, Bonds became the Giants' second-round selection in the 1982 June Amateur Draft, but Bonds and the Giants could not agree on a contract, so he opted to attend Arizona State on a baseball scholarship.

He continued to thrive while playing for the Sun Devils, where he hit .347 with 45 home runs and 175 RBIs during his stay in Tempe, Arizona. College baseball only enhanced his value to the professional ranks, prompting the Pittsburgh Pirates to make him the sixth overall pick of the 1985 draft. This time he signed.

By 1986 Bonds arrived in the major leagues, hitting 16 home runs and driving in 48 during his rookie campaign. In Bonds' first full season in the major leagues in 1987, he hit 25 home runs while also showing his versatility with 32 steals. He helped turn around the fortunes of a dismal Pirates franchise, leading the team to the

Barry Bonds watches his record-breaking 73rd home run of the season against the Los Angeles Dodgers on October 7, 2001.

postseason in 1990 while winning his first Most Valuable Player award after hitting .301 with 33 home runs and 114 RBIs.

Bonds would lead the Pirates to the postseason the following two seasons as well—capturing his second MVP in 1992—before he opted to leave the Pirates via free agency, signing a six-year deal with the Giants worth $43.75 million. Giants fans loved Bonds, whereas fans around the league perceived him as a villain.

Bonds wore his father's No. 25 and, in his first season with the team in 1993, led the Giants to the brink of the playoffs. The National and American Leagues were still divided into just two divisions, and the Giants' division included the Atlanta Braves. While the Giants won 103 games in 1993, the Braves won 104 to win the division and advance to the postseason. Bonds led the league in home runs with 46, and RBIs with 123, en route to another MVP award.

Over the years, Bonds' legend would grow the longer he played with the Giants, and he would grow, too, which supported allegations that he used performance-enhancing drugs. Despite the finger-pointing, his excellence continued on the field.

In 2001 Bonds clubbed 73 home runs to set the single-season home run mark. A methodical nationwide countdown then began that observed Bonds' pursuit of career home run leader Hank Aaron's mark of 755 home runs. Bonds surpassed that mark in 2007 to become the all-time home run king with 762 career home runs. In addition to Bonds' brilliance with the bat, he won eight Gold Gloves during his career.

He has been out of baseball since 2007 and under scrutiny in the midst of the steroid scandal and ensuing investigations. In 2007 Bonds was indicted for allegedly lying to the grand jury during the government's investigation of BALCO (Bay Area Laboratory Co-Operative). During Bonds' testimony, he told the grand jury he had never knowingly taken steroids.

In 15 seasons with the Giants, Bonds hit 586 home runs while knocking in 1,440 runs and posting a .312 batting average.

5 The Shot Heard Round the World

Ralph Waldo Emerson penned his poem "Concord Hymn" in 1837 and coined the phrase "the shot heard round the world" in reference to an episode from the American Revolutionary War. Since then, Emerson's phrase has been employed to describe various dramatic events in history. Baseball fans know the phrase well, as well as the participants, as they pertain to the events of October 3, 1951.

Bobby Thomson hits his "Shot Heard Round the World," a dotted line indicating the ball's flight over the left-field wall. Photo courtesy of AP Images

The Dodgers and Giants finished the 1951 season in a tie for first place with identical 96–58 records, which resulted in a best-of-three playoff series for the National League pennant.

Bobby Thomson was the hero of Game 1, which took place at Brooklyn's Ebbets Field, when he hit a two-run homer off Ralph Branca that proved to be the difference in a 3–1 Giants win. Dodgers rookie Clem Labine shut out the Giants in the second game, as the Dodgers' bats came alive in a 10–0 rout at the Polo Grounds to even the series and force a deciding third game.

Both teams had their ace on the hill for Game 3, which took place at the Polo Grounds with Sal Maglie going for the Giants and Don Newcombe for the Dodgers. The Dodgers got busy early when Jackie Robinson drove home Pee Wee Reese in the first inning to stake the Dodgers to a 1–0 lead.

Thomson answered for the Giants with a sacrifice fly in the bottom of the seventh to tie the game at 1. But in the top of the eighth, the Dodgers scored three runs against Maglie to give the Giants' hated rivals a 4–1 lead heading into the final half inning.

Heart had defined the Giants' journey throughout the 1951 season, which saw them catch the Dodgers after trailing by a large

Russ Hodges

Russ Hodges was known as the voice of the Giants for 22 seasons, from 1949 to 1970. Hailing from Dayton, Tennessee, Hodges began his broadcasting career in 1934. Prior to joining the Giants' crew, he worked for the Chicago Cubs, Washington Senators, and Cincinnati Reds. He then went to New York City, where he did home games for the New York Yankees and New York Giants.

When the Giants and Yankees separated their broadcasts in 1949 so each could broadcast a 154-game schedule, Hodges became the Giants' voice exclusively. "Bye-bye, baby!" became Hodges' signature home run call. His most famous moment came on October 3, 1951, when he called Bobby Thomson's "Shot Heard Round the World" home run that won the Giants the 1951 National League pennant. Not all broadcasts were recorded in the 1950s, and Hodges' signature broadcast almost was lost. Fortunately, a Dodgers fan had tape-recorded the moment, hoping to hear Hodges lamenting a Giants loss. The next day he called Hodges to tell him that he had recorded the historic moment and gave him the tape.

Hodges also called the Pabst Blue Ribbon Bouts on CBS from 1948 to 1955, and he was at the microphone for the second Muhammad Ali–Sonny Liston fight, which turned out to be one of the most controversial fights in boxing history. Hodges further demonstrated his versatility by broadcasting college and pro football games at different times during his career. He won the Ford C. Frick Award for broadcast excellence presented by the Baseball Hall of Fame in 1980. He died in 1971.

margin. Compared to what they had overcome, three runs in the ninth hardly seemed insurmountable.

Alvin Dark singled to start the Giants' ninth, and Don Mueller followed with a single to right field, which allowed Dark to get to third. Monte Irvin popped out for the first out of the inning before Whitey Lockman kept the inning alive when he slashed a double down the left-field line to drive home Dark and send Mueller to third. When Mueller slid, he hit the bag and broke his ankle, prompting Clint Hartung to be inserted as a pinch runner.

With Newcombe tiring, Dodgers manager Charlie Dressen lifted the right-hander and called for Branca, a move many questioned, considering the fact that Thomson was the next hitter and had homered off Branca in the first game. Why didn't Dressen call on Carl Erskine? Erskine had been warming up alongside Branca in the bullpen, but did not look sharp. Based on that information, Dressen opted to use Branca.

He delivered a fastball that Thomson watched for strike one. At 3:58 PM, Thomson swung at the next pitch, a fastball high and inside, and made solid contact, riding the ball down the left-field line. At first, the ball appeared as though it would bounce off the wall, but instead it cleared the wall for the game-winning round-tripper.

Giants broadcaster Russ Hodges then made his famous call over the radio as he watched the scene unfold: "There's a long drive…it's gonna be…I believe—the Giants win the pennant! The Giants win the pennant! The Giants win the pennant! The Giants win the pennant! Bobby Thomson hits into the lower deck of the left-field stands! The Giants win the pennant, and they're going crazy, they're going crazy!… I don't believe it, I don't believe it, I do not believe it!"

To Thomson's dying day he was remembered for his home run off Branca. "I can remember feeling as if time was just frozen," Thomson said of the blast. "It was a delirious, delicious moment."

6 2010: Wonderful Torture

Duane Kuiper came up with the phrase "Giants Torture" as a way for the longtime Giants broadcaster to describe the emotion of being a Giants fan during the 2010 season. That was when close games, featuring excruciating losses and exquisite victories, defined the team en route to the franchise's first World Series championship since 1954 and the first title for San Francisco after the team moved there from New York in 1958.

The team got off to a modest beginning, going 13–9 in April, 14–14 in May, and 13–14 in June before catching fire in July and going 20–8. Along the way, general manager Brian Sabean continued to augment the team by picking up players, the likes of which manager Bruce Bochy referred to fondly as "misfits."

Aubrey Huff was signed before the season, Pat Burrell came on board in May, Cody Ross and Jose Guillen came aboard in August, and all contributed significantly. Sabean's plan all along was to try and cobble together some sort of lineup that could support the best pitching staff in baseball, boasting starters Tim Lincecum, Matt Cain, and Jonathan Sanchez, along with closer Brian Wilson. Miraculously, the plan came together and blended into a marvelous chemistry that worked.

After experiencing a losing August in which the team went 13–15, the Giants faced an uphill battle if they wanted to displace the first-place San Diego Padres, who owned a four-game lead in the National League West. That set the stage for a September and October to remember in San Francisco.

In the last month of the season, the Giants charged to a 18–8 mark heading into the final weekend of the season, when all they

Rally Thong

Baseball is perhaps the sport most prone to superstitions. Players will do almost anything if they feel it can help their luck or the luck of the team—remember Mark Grace and "the slumpbuster?" But let's not go there.

Enter Aubrey Huff, who came up with what was likely a first at the end of the 2010 season when he employed the use of a "rally thong." Huff began wearing a lacy red thong, which he proudly modeled while strolling around the Giants clubhouse before and after games. To the credit of the Giants first baseman, he took one for the team by employing the somewhat different choice of underwear beginning with 30 games left on the 2010 schedule. To Huff's way of thinking, this was strictly a team gesture—he did not begin the practice to end a batting slump, he did so to give the team good luck. And he figured that the rally thong would be worth at least 20 wins in the Giants' final 30 games, which would therefore lead the team to a National League West title. The club got off to a 3–1 start with Huff in the rally thong, and he began to gain believers in the power of the thong.

Huff has always been known for his clubhouse antics and has never minded making himself the object of the joke. One can only imagine how ridiculous Huff looked talking to reporters wearing only his thong—actually, one would probably not want to imagine such a sight. Given the results, Giants fans would probably declare Huff the fashion plate of recent Giants teams. On August 30 the Giants trailed the first-place San Diego Padres by five games. The next night Huff went with his new look, and over the final 30 games of the season, the Giants won 20 to win the division just as Huff forecast.

That was one powerful thong.

needed was to win one game against the Padres to clinch the National League West. Instead, they lost the first two games, which left an interesting scenario heading into the final day of the season. If San Diego won the game, the Giants, Atlanta Braves, and Padres would all have identical 91–71 records, which would have forced a tiebreaker game on the Monday following the regular season to determine the winner of the National League West. The loser would then have to play the Braves to see which team would advance to the playoffs as the NL wild-card.

The Giants settled the issue in game 162, however, when they defeated the Padres 3–0 to win the division in front of an AT&T

Park crowd of 42,822 happy fans. The Giants then faced the Braves in the National League Division Series, and Ross led the way in Game 4 to pave the way for a 3–1 series victory. In that deciding game, Ross hit a solo home run off Braves starter Derek Lowe that broke up a no-hitter and tied the game. Then he delivered the game-winning hit when he singled in the seventh.

By advancing, the Giants moved ahead to play the defending National League–champion Philadelphia Phillies in the National League Championship Series. Ross built on his success in the NLDS by coming up big against the Phillies. In 20 at-bats, he hit .350 with three home runs, three doubles, and five RBIs to win

The Giants celebrate their 3–1 victory in Game 5 to win the World Series four games to one over the Texas Rangers on November 1, 2010, at Rangers Ballpark in Arlington, Texas.

NLCS MVP honors as the Giants took the series 4–2 to earn a place in the Fall Classic.

Ross drew the spotlight for his work in the NLCS, but there were plenty of heroes wearing Giants uniforms, particularly the pitching staff led by Lincecum and Cain, who continued to mow down opposing hitters.

The Giants faced the Texas Rangers in the World Series, hosting Games 1 and 2 at AT&T Park. Game 1 featured what most figured would be a pitching duel between Rangers ace Cliff Lee and Lincecum. During the 2010 playoffs, Lee had breezed through the batting orders of the Tampa Bay Rays and the New York Yankees, compiling a 3–0 record with a 0.75 ERA. During his career, he owned a 7–0 record in eight postseason starts. In short, the Texas left-hander appeared to be unbeatable. Some of the pundits even went so far as to call him the best playoff pitcher ever. Yes, he looked that invincible. That is, until he toed the rubber at AT&T Park.

The Giants hitters took care of business and came away with an 11–7 win. The next night Cain pitched for the Giants, and again the Giants routed the Rangers, this time by the score of 9–0 to send the Series to Texas with the Giants needing just two wins to complete their miraculous postseason run. Texas took the third game 4–2, but the Giants bounced back to shut out the Rangers 4–0 in Game 4, behind a solid pitching effort from rookie Madison Bumgarner.

Lincecum got the start in Game 5 and was lights out through eight innings, allowing only a solo home run to Nelson Cruz in the seventh while holding the Rangers to three hits. Series MVP Edgar Renteria came through with a three-run homer off Lee in the top of the seventh that gave the Giants all the offense they needed, as Wilson retired the Rangers in order in the ninth to preserve the win and earn the Giants their first World Series championship in San Francisco.

Giants fans will always fondly remember the 2010 season—it brought the most wonderful kind of torture.

7 Juan Marichal

Any kid growing up in the 1960s remembers the high leg kick—it belonged to Juan Marichal. The Giants right-hander's delivery was unique. When he went into his windup, he finished with a high leg kick that resembled something seen at a martial arts tournament. His left leg would go almost vertical. The purpose of the high kick was primarily to help disguise what pitch he was throwing to the plate, leaving the hitters guessing at what might arrive from his extensive repertoire.

When Marichal made his major league debut on July 19, 1960, he caught everyone's attention from the get-go by taking a no-hitter into the eighth inning before Clay Dalrymple hit a two-out single. Marichal did not allow another hit in the game and finished with a one-hit shutout in which he allowed one walk and struck out 12.

Marichal made 11 starts in his rookie season and went 6–2 with a 2.66 ERA. After making 63 starts the next two seasons and going 31–21, he had his breakout season in 1963 when he went 25–8 with a 2.41 ERA and 248 strikeouts. After the 1963 season, the Giants could bank on Marichal winning 20 games a season, which he did six out of seven years from 1963 to 1969. Twice he led the league in wins, in 1963 and in 1968, when he won 26 games.

The secret for a pitcher to win a lot of baseball games is not allowing the other team to score many runs. And Marichal was as stingy as any pitcher in baseball when it came to keeping opposing teams off the scoreboard, as evidenced by his finishing in the top 10 in ERA every year from 1963 to 1969.

To imagine Marichal's dominance, consider the fact he led the league in shutouts twice, including the 1965 season when he threw

Juan Marichal in his signature windup during a game at Candlestick Park in 1960. He was inducted into the Hall of Fame after compiling a career record of 243–142 with a 2.89 ERA in 16 major league seasons.

10. His best season came in 1969 when, in addition to going 21–11, he posted a 2.10 ERA. Control fueled Marichal's dominance throughout his career. In 16 major league seasons, he struck out 2,303 while walking just 709 for an incredible strikeout-to-walk ratio of 3.25-to-1.

While Marichal pitched many gems, two of the most memorable came in 1963. Marichal pitched a no-hitter against Houston on June 15, 1963, at Candlestick Park. Not even a month later, on July 2, 1963, he hooked up with Milwaukee Braves ace Warren Spahn in a pitching duel and came away a 1–0 winner after pitching 16 scoreless innings.

Despite all of Marichal's greatness, he had the misfortune of playing in an era that also included Sandy Koufax and Bob Gibson, which was akin to being a great player in the NBA during the years when Michael Jordan played. Their greatness often overshadowed his. Marichal's legacy also suffered due to an incident that occurred

Giants' 20-Game Winners

Christy Mathewson became the Giants' first 20-game winner of the 20th century in 1901 when he went 20–17. Before his career was complete, he would have 13 20-win seasons on his résumé, far and away the most 20-win seasons in Giants history. Twenty-eight other pitchers in the history of the franchise would win at least 20 games in a season. Amazingly, not since John Burkett went 22–7 and Billy Swift went 21–8 in 1993 have the Giants had a 20-game winner.

Here are the Giants pitchers who had at least one 20-win season:

Leon Ames	Mike McCormick
Johnny Antonelli	Joe McGinnity
Jess Barnes	Cliff Melton
Larry Benton	Art Nehf
Ron Bryant	Gaylord Perry
John Burkett	Jack Sanford
Fred Fitzsimmons	Hal Schumacher
Carl Hubbell	Ferdie Schupp
Larry Jansen	Billy Swift
Sam Jones	Luther Taylor
Mike Krukow	Jeff Tesreau
Sal Maglie	Fred Toney
Juan Marichal	Bill Voiselle
Rube Marquard	George Wiltse
Christy Mathewson	

in 1965 when he struck Dodgers catcher John Roseboro on the head with a bat (see No. 26, "John Roseboro Incident"). For many years after that, Marichal was vilified.

Marichal played 14 seasons for the Giants, posting a 238–140 record with a 2.84 ERA. He finished his career by playing for the Boston Red Sox in 1974 and the Dodgers in 1975, but he made just 13 total appearances. After he threw his last pitch in 1975, Marichal could look in the rearview mirror and see 243 wins and 142 losses, including an incredible 244 complete games. He made nine National League All-Star teams and was voted the Most Valuable Player of the 1965 game. In 1983 Marichal was inducted into the Baseball Hall of Fame. Today a statue of Marichal stands at AT&T Park that shows his unique pitching motion.

 **Bill Terry**

Bill Terry stood out as a pitcher as a young prospect, but nobody could have known he would end up being a Hall of Fame first baseman. At the age of 16, Terry, a native of Atlanta, made his professional baseball debut playing for minor league teams in the South starting in 1915, putting up some impressive numbers on the mound and giving every indication that pitching would be the left-hander's destiny. But the longer he played, the more his skills in the field and at the plate began to show through.

In 1922 the Toledo Mud Hens of the American Association brought Terry into the fold as a pitcher and a hitter. But facing a higher grade of hitters brought his pitching numbers back to earth—he went 9–9 in 26 games for the Mud Hens. Meanwhile his numbers with a bat in his hands just seemed to get better, as he hit 14 homers with a .336 batting average.

Terry spent another season in Toledo in 1923, but this time he played first base only. He continued to thrive, hitting .377 with 15 home runs in 109 games, which caught the Giants' attention. They purchased Terry on September 18, 1923, and six days later he made his major league debut, his first at-bat coming as a pinch-hitter against the Cincinnati Reds.

In 1924 Terry played in 77 games for the Giants, backing up George Kelly at first base. His numbers at the end of the season were hardly attention-grabbing, as he hit just .239 with five home runs and 24 RBIs. But in the World Series, he hit .429 with a home run against Washington Senators ace Walter Johnson.

Heinie Groh got injured early in the 1925 season, causing a reshuffling of the lineup in the field, including a move that saw Kelly go from first base to second. This shift allowed Terry to take over at first base. He took advantage of the opportunity, hitting .319 with 11 home runs and 70 RBIs. Despite the results, Terry did not win the job and again backed up Kelly in 1926, in addition to playing some outfield. By the end of the season, Terry had a .289 average with five home runs and 43 RBIs in 98 games.

The Giants management was active in the off-season prior to the 1927 season, and the trades they made resulted in Terry taking over at first base. Once again, he took advantage of his opportunity, hitting .326 with 20 home runs and 121 RBIs. After that season, the Giants left Terry alone, and he took care of business. Terry followed in 1928 with another .326 season before jumping up to .372 in 1929, and then hitting .401 in 1930, making him the first player since Rogers Hornsby to hit .400. To date, Terry's .401 season remains the last time a National League player hit .400 or above. In addition, Terry had 254 hits, which is still tied for the National League record for the most hits in a season.

In 1932 he succeeded John McGraw as player/manager, taking over during a season that saw the Giants finish in sixth place. The

Giants Hit .319

Imagine hitting .319 for a season—as a team. Hard to imagine, but the Giants finished the 1930 season with a .319 batting average. Of course, having a hitter who bats .401—which Bill Terry did that season—goes a long way toward establishing that mark.

Hughie Critz and Wally Roettger must have felt like outsiders on the 1930 Giants squad after hitting .265 and .283, respectively. Virtually every other Giants regular hit .300 or higher. Fred Lindstrom hit .379; Mel Ott hit .349; and Shanty Hogan and Travis Jackson each hit .339. Even the pitchers got into the action with the sticks, as Freddie Fitzsimmons hit .265, and Clarence Mitchell hit .255. All told, the Giants had 10 players who hit .300 or better. The Giants' .319 team batting average led the National League in hitting during a season that saw them score 959 runs. Unfortunately for the team, the offensive assault did not translate to a National League pennant, as the team finished in third place.

Of course, the 1930 season is remembered as the most offensive season in major league history. Terry led the league in hitting, and Babe Herman finished second at .393, the highest mark by any hitter in major league history who finished second in the league in hitting. Hack Wilson had 191 RBIs that season, and the St. Louis Cardinals and New York Yankees each scored more than 1,000 runs. Meanwhile the Philadelphia Phillies, who finished the season in last place, hit .315, which was .001 higher as a team than the first-place Cardinals. For the season, 71 players hit over .300 in 1930.

following season Terry guided the Giants to the National League pennant and a World Series championship.

Terry's final season as a player came in 1936, when he closed out his 14-year career with a .310 average at the age of 37. He finished with a .341 lifetime batting average, 154 home runs, and 1,078 RBIs. He led the team to a second consecutive pennant in 1937—losing once again to the Yankees in the World Series—and managed the Giants until 1941. In 1954 Terry was inducted into the Baseball Hall of Fame, and today his retired No. 3 Giants uniform is posted on the façade of the upper deck in the left-field corner of AT&T Park. Terry died on January 9, 1989, in Jacksonville, Florida, at the age of 90.

9 The Catch

One play can define an entire World Series, and that's what happened during the 1954 Fall Classic between the Giants and the Cleveland Indians when Willie Mays made a play that came to be known simply as "the Catch."

The Giants went into the '54 Series as decided underdogs to the Indians, who had set a modern record by winning 111 games and losing just 43. On September 29, 1954, the first game of the 1954 World Series was played in New York at the Polo Grounds. With the score tied at 2 in the top of the eighth, Giants starter Sal Maglie got into trouble. First he issued a walk to Larry Doby, and Al Rosen followed with a single. Leo Durocher had seen enough, so the Giants manager decided to play the percentages by bringing in left-hander Don Liddle to pitch to left-handed-hitting Vic Wertz. Liddle fell behind in the count 2–1. Wertz then swung at Liddle's fourth pitch, making solid contact to send a drive to deep center field some 460 feet away. Had Wertz hit a similar drive in most any other major league ballpark, he would have been making a leisurely stroll around the bases, since the ball would have cleared the wall for a three-run homer.

Instead, the drive set off a moment in which every fan in the ballpark held his or her breath, wondering if by some miracle Giants center fielder Willie Mays could cover enough ground to reach the baseball before it hit the ground. Mays gave chase and, at the last instant, hauled in the drive, making an over-the-shoulder catch like a wide receiver catching a deep pass after pulling away from a defender. Once Mays had the ball in his possession, he whirled and made a throw to the infield, losing his hat in the

A breakdown of Willie Mays making "the Catch" on a long drive by the Indians' Vic Wertz in the eighth inning of Game 1 in the 1954 World Series.

process. Doby would have easily scored from second base had he tagged up on the play, but Doby, like most everybody else in the ballpark, did not think Mays could make the catch. So he had taken off, only to return to second base, which he tagged, and managed to get to third. Thus the Indians scored no runs on the play, leaving runners on first and third with one out.

Durocher then brought in Marv Grissom to relieve Liddle, who was said to quip to Grissom, "Well, I got my man!" Grissom walked the next hitter to load the bases, but he retired the next two to end the inning without any runs scoring.

In the bottom of the 10th inning, the Giants went on to win when pinch-hitter Dusty Rhodes hit a three-run homer off Indians starter Bob Lemon to give the Giants a 5–2 win. In a bitter pill for the Indians to swallow, Rhodes' drive cleared the wall at the shortest point of the Polo Grounds, which was at right field some 260 feet from home plate.

The Giants went on to sweep the World Series, which many attributed to the momentum-changing catch made by Mays. Over the years, many have questioned how great a catch Mays had made. Others maintained that, had the catch been made in a city other than New York by a player from a team not from New York, it might not be considered one of the greatest in major league history. Even Mays felt like the catch was overrated, which he has said in interviews many times. However, based on the timing—at a pivotal moment of Game 1—and the actual catch that was made, it is hard to dispute its brilliance.

To see "the Catch" for yourself, just go to YouTube and type in: "Willie Mays the Catch."

10 Orlando Cepeda

Orlando Cepeda's first season in the major leagues set the template for a Hall of Fame career when the 20-year-old from Puerto Rico hit .312 with 25 home runs and 96 RBIs. For his performance, Cepeda was named the National League's 1958 Rookie of the Year. Nobody from Puerto Rico was surprised at Cepeda's success since his father, Pedro, had been a highly successful professional baseball player in Puerto Rico. Orlando grew up watching his father play and looking forward to the day he would be old enough and strong enough to ply the family trade.

In Cepeda's second season, the Giants moved him from first to third base to make room for Willie McCovey. The move did not work out for Cepeda, who had trouble fielding the hot corner, and it eventually prompted a move to the outfield. Despite his struggles with the glove, Cepeda continued to hit, avoiding the sophomore jinx with a .317 average, 27 home runs, and 105 RBIs. Cepeda's steady offensive performance continued in his third season, which saw the Giants move Cepeda back to first base after McCovey was sent to the minor leagues. Cepeda finished that 1960 campaign with a .297 batting average, complimented by 24 home runs and 96 RBIs. Cepeda is among five players in major league history to have hit 20-plus home runs and 30-plus doubles in each of his first three major league seasons. The others are Albert Pujols, Joe DiMaggio, Ted Williams, and Evan Longoria.

In Cepeda's fourth season, he elevated his performance to the best year of his career when he hit .311 and led the league in home runs (46) and RBIs (142). That excellence continued through the 1964 season, despite a troubling knee injury that kept him in constant pain. In 1965 the injury finally reared its ugly head to the point that it affected his performance. He had only 40 at-bats in 1965 and hit just .176.

Figuring they had plenty of firepower in McCovey and Mays, and believing that Cepeda was in a downward spiral due to his knee, the Giants traded Cepeda to the St. Louis Cardinals for left-hander Ray Sadecki 19 games into the 1966 season. In nine seasons with the Giants, Cepeda hit .308 with 226 home runs and 767 RBIs.

He played for the Cardinals from 1966 to 1968, winning Most Valuable Player honors in 1967 when the Cardinals won the World Series. He would then have tours of duty with the Atlanta Braves (1969–1972), Oakland Athletics (1972), Boston Red Sox (1973), and Kansas City Royals (1974) before retiring after the 1974 season. Over 17 major league seasons, Cepeda hit .297 with 379

Giants first baseman/outfielder Orlando Cepeda takes a cut during a game. Named Rookie of the Year in 1958, he made the All-Star team his next six seasons with the Giants. In his 17-year, Hall of Fame career, Cepeda collected 2,351 hits, smashed 379 homers, and drove in 1,365 runs.

home runs and 1,365 RBIs. "Cha-Cha" was a seven-time All-Star during his career and earned the distinction as the first player from Puerto Rico to start in the mid-summer classic.

After being convicted of drug possession charges in 1978, Cepeda received a five-year prison sentence, of which he served 10 months, with the rest on probation. That notoriety delayed his election to the Hall of Fame, but in 1999 the Veterans Committee inducted Cepeda into the Hall. By entering the Hall of Fame, Cepeda became only the second player from Puerto Rico (Roberto Clemente being the first) to do so.

Cepeda's No. 30 jersey was retired by the Giants on July 11, 1999. The man known as "the Baby Bull" currently works for the Giants as a community ambassador, a role that sees him go into the community to visit at-risk children in inner-city schools.

Mel Ott

Crossword aficionados are familiar with Mel Ott, but the Hall of Famer was far more than a major league player with a three-letter last name. By the time Ott's 22-year career had run its course, the native of Gretna, Louisiana, had become the first National League player to exceed 500 career home runs.

Ott batted left-handed and played outfield for the Giants. Though a mighty power hitter, he never looked the part, standing just 5'9", 170 pounds. Ott employed a unique batting style that would see him lift his front foot prior to taking his swing. Unusual as Ott's swing looked, it likely explained how he was able to generate enough bat speed to produce the home runs he did.

He arrived to the major leagues in 1926 at the age of 17 to play for John McGraw's Giants. He played in just 117 games for the Giants in 1926 and 1927 before becoming a regular in 1928. At the age of 19, Ott played in 124 games, hitting .322 with 18 home runs and 77 RBIs. From there, he flourished, hitting .315 with a .557 slugging percentage, and collecting 1,939 hits, 342 home runs, 1,306 RBIs, and 1,035 walks all before he turned 30. In 1929 Ott broke out with 42 home runs and 151 RBIs while hitting .328. He finished second in the league in home runs behind Philadelphia's Chuck Klein, which brought along a healthy dose of controversy. Philadelphia and New York played a doubleheader at the end of the season in which the Phillies pitchers opted to walk Ott every time he came up in order to keep him from tying their teammate.

While Ott did not claim a home run title the year he hit his career high, he did go on to lead the National League in home runs six times, including the 1942 season when he hit 30 home runs at the age of 33. In addition to doing a superlative job playing right field, Ott played third base for the Giants from 1937 to 1938 when the team needed a third baseman.

During his career, the Giants won three National League pennants, and Ott played a large part in winning the 1933 World Series. Not only did Ott open the Series in style with a first-inning

Mel Ott, shown in his rookie season, played for the New York Giants from 1926 to 1947, posting a .304 lifetime average, 511 home runs, and 1,860 RBIs, on his way to induction into the Hall of Fame.

home run in Game 1, he also helped close the Series in just the right way with a home run in the 10th inning of Game 5, which put the Giants over the top. At the end of the Series, Ott had a .389 average with seven hits and four RBIs to complement his home runs.

In 1937 Ott moved past Rogers Hornsby to become the all-time National League home run king. Willie Mays took over that spot in 1966. But Ott's value as a contributor on offense could not be measured in home runs alone. He became the first National League player to accrue eight straight 100-RBI seasons, which he did from 1929 to 1936. Since then, Willie Mays, Sammy Sosa, Chipper Jones, and Albert Pujols are the only National League hitters to accomplish the feat.

Of note, he still ranks as the youngest major leaguer to hit for the cycle as he achieved the rare baseball feat on May 16, 1929, at the age of 20. Good things happened when Ott swung the bat, and things happened even when he didn't. He often reached base via the base on balls. Four times he collected five walks in a game, and he set a National League record for the most walks in a doubleheader when he walked six times on October 5, 1929. Ten times during his career he walked at least 100 times in a season, and he led the National League in walks six times.

Ott managed the Giants from 1942 to 1948. He remained active as a player for all of his years as a manager but 1948. He could never be accused of not having a sense of humor, which was reflected in this quote about his three-letter last name when he said, "Every time I sign a ball, and there have been thousands, I thank my luck that I wasn't born [Stan] Coveleski or [Bill] Wambsganss or [Roger] Peckinpaugh."

He finished his career with a .304 average, 511 home runs, 1,860 RBIs, 2,876 hits, and 1,708 walks. In 1951 Ott was elected to the Baseball Hall of Fame. The Giants retired his No. 4 in 1949.

Willie McCovey

Few players in major league history struck fear in the opposition like "Stretch" once did. Willie McCovey would step into the batter's box, and defenders would immediately think about self-preservation. Disturbing thoughts followed about what might happen if the 6'4", 200-pound Giants first baseman used his powerful left-handed cut to unleash a drive in their direction.

Longtime Los Angeles Dodgers manager Walter Alston said of him, "McCovey didn't hit any cheap one[s]. When he belts a home run, he does it with such authority, it seems like an act of God. You can't cry about it."

McCovey sparkled in his Giants debut on July 30, 1959, when he went 4-for-4 against Robin Roberts, the Philadelphia Phillies' Hall of Fame right-hander. By the end of the season, McCovey had a .354 batting average with 13 home runs and 38 RBIs; along the way he cobbled together a 22-game hitting streak. Despite playing in just 52 games, the native of Mobile, Alabama, won National League Rookie of the Year honors.

McCovey did not become an everyday player until 1963. Prior to that season, he was best known as the guy with unlimited potential who lined out with two on to end the 1962 World Series (see No. 17, "The One That Got Away"). But McCovey would have his coming-out party in 1963 when he hit .280 with 44 home runs and 102 RBIs. He would become a cog in the Giants' batting order, providing a left-handed power complement to right-handed hitting sluggers Willie Mays and Orlando Cepeda.

McCovey put together his best season in 1969 when he hit .320 with 45 home runs and 126 RBIs. The home run and RBI totals

Willie McCovey takes off for first base after connecting on a drive during a game in 1961. McCovey broke out in 1963 and tore the league up in 1969, his MVP season. He clubbed 521 home runs during his Hall of Fame career.

led the league, while his batting average ranked fifth, leaving him one leg shy of accomplishing baseball's Triple Crown. And, keep in mind, those numbers were accrued during a dominant pitching era. McCovey earned MVP honors for his 1969 work.

Prior to the 1974 season, the Giants traded McCovey to the San Diego Padres, where he played for parts of three seasons before going to the Oakland Athletics during the 1976 season. He played 11 games for the A's before returning to the Giants in 1977 at the age of 39. That became an eventful season for McCovey and Giants

Willie Mac Award

Willie McCovey played 19 seasons for the Giants during two tours with the team. For his work between the lines, McCovey was inducted into the Baseball Hall of Fame in 1986. While McCovey obviously brought great talents to the playing field, what he did on the diamond paled in comparison to the kind of teammate he was, the kind of leadership he showed, and the first-class human being he was when not playing baseball. Thus, the Willie Mac Award came into being beginning in 1980 in honor of McCovey. The award is presented annually to the Giants player who best exemplifies the spirit and leadership that McCovey showed throughout his career. The award is voted upon by the Giants players and coaching staff.

Each winner's name is commemorated with a plaque in the ground that surrounds the statue of Willie McCovey on the southern shore of China Basin, unofficially known as McCovey Cove. Here are the winners since the inception of the award:

1980	Jack Clark	1996	Shawon Dunston
1981	Larry Herndon	1997	J.T. Snow
1982	Joe Morgan	1998	Jeff Kent
1983	Darrell Evans	1999	Marvin Benard
1984	Bob Brenly	2000	Ellis Burks
1985	Mike Krukow	2001	Mark Gardner and
1986	Mike Krukow		Benito Santiago
1987	Chris Speier	2002	David Bell
1988	Jose Uribe	2003	Marquis Grissom
1989	Dave Dravecky	2004	J.T. Snow
1990	Steve Bedrosian	2005	Mike Matheny
1991	Robby Thompson	2006	Omar Vizquel
1992	Mike Felder	2007	Bengie Molina
1993	Kirt Manwaring	2008	Bengie Molina
1994	*(not awarded due to strike)*	2009	Matt Cain
1995	Mark Leiter and	2010	Andres Torres
	Mark Carreon		

fans, who got to experience the joy of having him back on the team. During that season, McCovey became the first player in major league history to hit two home runs in one inning twice. Prior to accomplishing the feat on June 27, 1977, against the Cincinnati

Reds, McCovey had turned the trick on April 12, 1973. In addition, one of the home runs was a grand slam, giving McCovey 17 for his career, which established a National League record at the time. McCovey finished the 1977 season with a .280 batting average with 28 home runs and 86 RBIs to earn National League Comeback Player of the Year honors.

McCovey hit his 500th home run the following season on June 30 against the Braves. In 1980 he played his final season, but he didn't retire before clubbing his 521st home run, which would be recognized as unique, since the blast meant he had homered in four different decades. Rickey Henderson and Ted Williams are the only players other than McCovey to accomplish the feat.

In 19 seasons with the Giants, McCovey hit 469 home runs while driving in 1,388 and hitting .274. During his 22-year career, he recorded 521 home runs with 1,555 RBIs. He made six All-Star Games and had his No. 44 retired by the Giants in 1975. In 1986 McCovey was inducted into the Baseball Hall of Fame.

Tim Lincecum

Tim Lincecum doesn't look the part. Most big-league pitchers have size, which generates the necessary juice to their fastballs, thus making them big-league fastballs. Lincecum never had the prerequisite size. He stands 5'11" and weighs 172 pounds. But what he lacks in size, he makes up for with his technique and repertoire of pitches. Included in his tool belt of pitches are a mid-90s fastball, a change-up, a curve, and a slider. Lincecum's technique and repertoire have allowed him to become one of the best pitchers in the major leagues almost from the first day he suited up for the Giants.

Tim Lincecum delivers to home plate during the fifth and deciding game of the 2010 World Series against the Texas Rangers in Arlington, Texas. Over eight innings, he allowed just three hits and one earned run, picking up the win.

The right-hander dazzled while in high school in Renton, Washington, prompting the Chicago Cubs to select him in the 48th round of the 2003 draft. He opted to attend the University of Washington, though, where he continued to dazzle. In his first year pitching for the Huskies, he won Pac-10 Freshman of the Year and Pitcher of the Year honors. He was drafted in 2005, this time by the Cleveland Indians, but again he did not sign. In 2006 he won the Golden Spikes Award—awarded to the top amateur baseball player for that season—when he went 12–4 with a 1.94 ERA and 199 strikeouts in 125⅓ innings. Not until the Giants chose him with the

10th pick of the 2006 draft did he sign a professional contract, which he did on June 30, 2006, agreeing to a deal that paid him a $2.025 million signing bonus.

After Russ Ortiz suffered an injury early in the 2007 season, Lincecum was called to the major leagues and made his first start on May 6, 2007, when he received a no-decision against the Philadelphia Phillies. He made his second career start on May 11, 2007, in Denver against the Colorado Rockies and came away with his first win after allowing two earned runs in seven innings. He would finish his rookie season with a 7–5 record and a 4.00 ERA in 24 starts.

In his second season in the major leagues, Lincecum continued to turn up the heat. In nine of his starts, he had double-digit strike-outs, finishing the season with 265 Ks to lead the National League, while posting an impressive record of 18–5, a 2.62 ERA, 227 innings pitched, and two complete games. At the end of the season, Lincecum was named the winner of the 2008 National League Cy Young Award. He became the first second-year player to win the award since the Kansas City Royals' Bret Saberhagen and New York Mets' Dwight Gooden won their respective leagues' Cy Young Awards in 1985.

In 2009 Lincecum again dominated National League hitters, posting a 15–7 record with 261 strikeouts in 225⅓ innings. Included in his body of work was the gem he pitched against the Pittsburgh Pirates on July 27 when he struck out a career-high 15, making him the first Giants pitcher to do so since Jason Schmidt turned the trick on June 6, 2006. Once again the Baseball Writers Association of America voted Lincecum as the winner of the National League Cy Young Award, earning him the distinction of being the first to win the Cy Young in his first two full seasons in the major leagues.

Lincecum did not have his best season in 2010, but he was at his best when it counted most, during the Giants' World Series run.

In September he went 5–1 with a 1.94 ERA in six starts before going 4–1 with a 2.43 ERA in six postseason appearances, including a stellar eight-inning performance in which he picked up the win in the deciding Game 5 of the World Series.

Lincecum is off to a tremendous start in his major league career and should give Giants fans plenty to cheer about in years to come.

14 The $30,000 Muff

During Fred Snodgrass' nine-year major league career, he was known as one of the best fielding outfielders in the National League. Sadly, the native of Ventura, California, is best remembered for a play he didn't make rather than all of the plays he made. Snodgrass had played in just 34 games in parts of two major league seasons prior to his first full season in 1910, when he burst onto the scene with a .321 average. Having earned a spot in John McGraw's outfield, Snodgrass played in the Giants' three consecutive World Series appearances in 1911, 1912, and 1913. What happened in the second of those appearances would stay with him for the rest of his life.

Fighting off the disappointment of losing to the Philadelphia Athletics in the 1911 World Series, the Giants showed their excellence again in 1912 by claiming their second straight National League pennant. They had expected to play the Athletics again, but the surprising Boston Red Sox had stormed to the pennant to interrupt any plans for revenge the Giants might have had. The pitching tandem of Christy Mathewson and Rube Marquard led the Giants' charges. Including a Game 2 that was called after 11 innings in a 6–6 tie, the Series was knotted at three games apiece and came down to a deciding Game 8 played at Boston's Fenway Park, with a crowd of 17,034 watching.

Mathewson had had his first start wiped away by the tie in Game 2 and lost his other start in Game 5, so McGraw's decision to start the future Hall of Famer brought out the second-guessers. But the choice of pitchers seemed to pay off as Mathewson held the Sox to one run through nine innings in another tie game. The Giants' offense finally got in gear in the top of the 10th, when Red Murray's one-out double set the table for Fred Merkle, who singled him home. So the Giants had their ace on the hill with a 2–1 lead heading into the bottom of the 10th inning, which prompted a raucous celebration by Giants fans in the enemy ballpark. That celebration quickly got silenced in the bottom half of the inning.

The Red Sox sent a pinch-hitter to the plate in Clyde Engle, who launched a towering fly ball toward center field. Snodgrass camped under the ball, ready to make the routine catch he normally made 100 times out of 100. But he dropped the ball, and by the time he retrieved it and got it back to the infield, Engle stood on second base, representing the tying run. Snodgrass' teammates stood in amazement, their mouths wide open.

Snodgrass appeared to be the most surprised person in the ballpark, and everyone could see that the Giants center fielder was upset. But he didn't let the unsettling nature of his error affect his performance. On the following play, Harry Hopper hit a line drive to center that looked like extra bases, but Snodgrass hauled it in with an acrobatic catch. While the catch had to be admired, it should have been for the second out rather than the first. Engle tagged at second and advanced to third on the play.

Mathewson then walked Steve Yerkes before Tris Speaker singled home Engle to tie the game at 2 and send Yerkes to third. McGraw instructed Mathewson to intentionally walk the next hitter, Duffy Lewis, to load the bases and set up the double play. Unfortunately for the Giants, Larry Gardner hit a sacrifice fly to right field that scored Yerkes and gave the Red Sox the championship. Deserving or not, Snodgrass became the goat of the World

Series, and the botched fly ball came to be known as "the $30,000 Muff," as that was the difference between the winning and losing team's shares for the World Series.

McGraw could be counted among those who did not blame Snodgrass for the Giants' loss as he wrote in his book, *Thirty Years in the Game*: "Often I have been asked what I did to Fred Snodgrass after he dropped that fly ball in the World Series of 1912.... I will tell you exactly what I did: I raised his salary $1,000." Snodgrass carried his legacy to the grave. When he died on April 5, 1974, his *New York Times'* obituary carried the headline, "Fred Snodgrass, 86, Dead; Ball Player Muffed 1912 Fly."

15 Candlestick Park

Candlestick Park was in the works as the future home of the Giants as soon as the team moved to San Francisco from New York following the 1957 season. In 1958 builders broke ground for the stadium known as the first modern stadium, based on the fact that the structure was composed entirely of reinforced concrete. The grand new ballpark opened its doors for business on April 12, 1960, on Opening Day with Richard Nixon throwing out the first pitch.

Candlestick Park is located on the western shore of San Francisco Bay, the site chosen primarily due to the availability and cost of the land. The ballpark took its name from Candlestick Point, the piece of land on which it sits and which sticks out into the Bay.

To everyone in baseball, Candlestick's reputation derived from the prevailing weather conditions that could affect any game at any moment. Not only did the wind swirl in every direction, there was fog, damp air, and often chilly temperatures. Needless to say, players struggled to catch fly balls, and hitters often felt like they needed a bazooka to hit a ball out of the park. Ironically, the initial design of the park did try to address the wind with the shape of the upper deck, but it ultimately failed to mitigate the wind's ill effects.

For those unaware of what misery playing in Candlestick could bring a ballplayer, they were enlightened during the 1961 All-Star Game, when a gust of wind knocked Giants pitcher Stu Miller off balance, which resulted in a balk being called. Another episode saw the batting cage lifted by the wind and dropped almost 100 feet from its initial position.

Giants owner Horace Stoneham had thought himself prudent by visiting the site for the ballpark during the day. But all it did was give him a false sense of security about the location. Had he thought to make such a visit at night, he would have discovered the demons that visited the park at night. Years later, Stoneham conducted a study of the problem, and the results revealed that, had the park been built several hundred yards to the east, the weather conditions would have been significantly better.

Understanding the severity of the weather and the adverse effect it had on attendance, the Giants made sure to schedule more day games than any other ballpark in the major leagues except Wrigley Field, which did not have lights until 1988.

The NFL's San Francisco 49ers moved in as co-tenants of the stadium, which prompted stands to be built around the outfield during the winter of 1971–1972. Many felt that the construction, which blocked the view of the Bay but also enclosed the stadium, would end the wind problem. It did not. The wind still made frequent visits to Candlestick Park in a swirling fashion.

Candlestick Park served as the host for two All-Star Games (1961 and 1984), a National League Division Series (1997), three National League Championship Series (1971, 1987, and 1989), and two World Series (1962 and 1989). The 1989 World Series, which saw the Giants face the Oakland Athletics, was disrupted by the Loma Prieta earthquake just prior to the start of Game 3 at Candlestick Park. The powerful quake did terrible damage to much of the Bay Area and put the Series on hold for 10 days before play was finally resumed.

The Giants relocated from Candlestick Park to PacBell Park (later changed to AT&T Park) in downtown San Francisco. The Giants' final game at Candlestick took place on September 30, 1999, and saw the Giants lose to the Dodgers 9–4.

Croix de Candlestick

Braving the cold of Candlestick Park had its merits. For starters, you were usually one of an elite collection of fans who decided that watching the Giants was worth packing every piece of warm clothing before heading to the ballpark. Cold winds swirled inside the park whether the game was in the day or at night. But games played after the sun went down were particularly brutal. Not only would the winds swirl, but those swirling winds were accompanied by frigid temperatures.

The Giants understood they had a legitimate problem to deal with, trying to lure customers into the icebox to watch the team play—especially at night. Given the nature of the beast, they tried to schedule as many games as possible when the sun was out. But there still were times when the schedule mandated that a night game be played. At the beginning of most night games, the sun could be counted on to shine through the early innings. But once the sun ducked down over the Pacific coast, the temperature inside the ballpark would drop. Out would come the earmuffs, gloves, parkas, and some fans even wore wetsuits underneath the clothes they were wearing; these were the hardcore fans prepared to brave the elements. Others were not as well-prepared.

Eventually, the temperature drop inside the 'Stick equated to gradual departures by most of the fans until the stands were close to empty by the ninth inning—even if the Giants were winning. Hoping to keep fans in the ballpark until the end of the games, in addition to looking for a way to reward those brave souls who remained at the games until the end, the Giants came up with the Croix de Candlestick pin. The pins were awarded to fans who stayed for the duration of an extra-inning night game, and they became a source of pride for Giants fans who were loyal enough to suffer until the end in order to watch their team. Fans today can still be seen wearing their pins to Giants game as a badge of honor.

16 The Polo Grounds

Prior to the Giants relocating from New York to San Francisco after the 1957 season, the Giants called the Polo Grounds home. Originally, the park was built in 1876 to be used as a field for the sport of polo. Over the years, the park would relocate and be rebuilt as it was used by a host of New York sports teams, including the Giants and the New York Yankees.

After moving from its original location at 110th Street, the final three versions of the Polo Grounds were located at the northwest corner of 155th Street and Eighth Avenue. Overlooking the ballpark to the north and west was a steep promontory called Coogan's Bluff, making the field's location Coogan's Hollow. On April 14, 1911, Polo Grounds III incurred a fire that burned down the grandstands, leaving only the supporting steel. The Giants shared Hilltop Park with the Yankees while the Polo Grounds were rebuilt. Amazingly, that reconstruction had advanced quickly enough to have the Giants move back into the park—in the form of its fourth version—on June 28, 1911.

Playing in their refurbished ballpark, the Giants won National League pennants in 1911, 1912, and 1913. The Giants owner, John T. Brush, made a failed attempt to change the name of the Polo Grounds to Brush Stadium, but the old name would not go away. Polo Grounds IV had a unique oblong shape with odd dimensions, such as the 483-foot distance to center field—which many estimated to be more like 505 feet.

No home runs were ever hit that cleared the center-field wall. At the same time, hitters could take shots at the short porches in left and right fields—279 and 258 feet, respectively—that were more than 200 feet closer. On top of that, a 21-foot overhang in left field often turned routine fly balls into home runs. Never was the quirky nature of the ballpark more apparent than during the first game of the 1954 World Series. In that game, Cleveland's Vic Wertz hit a ball to center field that would have been a home run in most major league ballparks. Instead, the drive turned into Willie Mays' amazing over-the-shoulder catch (see No. 9, "The Catch") and one of the longest fly-outs in World Series history. Meanwhile, Dusty Rhodes' game-winning home run went to right field and traveled about half as far as Wertz's drive. That contrast played to the Giants' favor as they swept the Indians to win the World Series.

When the Yankees' lease on Hilltop Park ran out, they worked out a deal with the Giants to sublet the Polo Grounds from 1913 to 1922. That arrangement ended in 1923 with the opening of Yankee Stadium—the "House That Ruth Built"—across the Harlem River from the Polo Grounds in the Bronx. Before the Yankees moved out, however, the home of both New York baseball teams hosted two World Series between the Yanks and the Giants in 1921 and 1922, the Giants beating their rivals both times. But with the Yankees in their new home in 1923, they finally beat the Giants in that year's Fall Classic.

By the late 1950s, the Polo Grounds had reached an age that prompted the Giants to bark about the need to have a new ballpark. When the Giants were unable to gain a deal for a new stadium in the New York area, they made the decision to move to San Francisco following the 1957 season. In their 75 years playing at the four different iterations of the Polo Grounds, the Giants won 17 National League pennants and five World Series championships.

Before dying its ultimate death, the Polo Grounds hosted the New York Titans of the fledgling American Football League and the expansion New York Mets. The City of New York claimed the land where the Polo Grounds stood in 1961, which allowed them to condemn the stadium. After a legal battle between the city and the

1921 Giants Snap Drought

When the Giants reached the World Series in 1921, they were riding a streak of four consecutive losses in the Fall Classic (1911–1913 and 1917). The Polo Grounds was the Giants' home field, and the Polo Grounds also served as home for the Yankees in 1921, so each of the eight games in the 1921 World Series was played there, making this the first World Series to have all of its games played at the same location.

Leading the way for the Giants were right fielder Ross Youngs, third baseman Frankie Frisch, left fielder Irish Meusel, and first baseman George "High Pockets" Kelly. Despite suffering from various arm and knee problems, Babe Ruth led the Yankees, bringing along the 59 home runs he hit during the season, which established a single-season home run mark. Manager John McGraw's "small ball" Giants pitted against Ruth's "long ball" Yankees proved to be an interesting contrast. The Yankees took the first two games by identical 3–0 scores. In Game 3, the script appeared to be the same when the Yankees took a 4–0 lead. The Giants showed some heart, however, overcoming the deficit and storming to a 13–5 victory. Ruth clubbed his first World Series home run in Game 4, but the Giants still took a 4–2 win to even the series. Ironically, Ruth used a bunt single to ignite a 3–1 Yankees win in Game 5.

Trailing 3–2 in the best-of-nine series, the Giants ran together two straight wins to take a 4–3 lead. Southpaw Art Nehf took the mound in Game 8 and finished the job for the Giants by pitching a four-hit shutout to give the Giants a 1–0 win over the Yankees and their first World Series championship since 1905.

Coogan Family, which still owned the property, the city won the battle, which eventually led to high-rise housing on the property where the Polo Grounds stood.

17 The One That Got Away

In the Giants' fifth year in San Francisco, they managed to put it all together, winning the National League pennant with a 103–62 record that included a three-game playoff defeat of the L.A. Dodgers to get into the World Series. Everything seemed to be going the Giants' way, which made the manner that the World Series ended out of character for the story line that had been playing out.

The Giants' opponent for the World Series was the defending-champion New York Yankees, who were headed to their 27th Fall Classic. Whitey Ford started Game 1 for the Yankees, and they took a 6–2 win. But the Giants' Jack Sanford tossed a 2–0 shutout in Game 2 to even the series. Roger Maris' two-run single in the seventh led the Yankees to a 3–2 win in Game 3; then Chuck Hiller, who'd had just 20 home runs in his eight-year major league career, hit a grand slam to lead the Giants to a win in Game 4. Tom Tresh hit a three-run homer to lead the Yankees to a win in Game 5 before both teams had to wait five days to play again due to travel and rain delays. Once they returned to play, Billy Pierce tossed a three-hitter for the Giants while Orlando Cepeda led the Giants' offense with a three-hit, two-RBI performance in a 5–2 win to force a deciding Game 7 at Candlestick Park.

Ralph Terry, who had gained notoriety in the minds of most Yankees fans for surrendering Bill Mazeroski's walk-off homer that ended the 1960 World Series, started Game 7 for the Yankees. He responded by holding the Giants scoreless on two hits through eight innings as the Yankees took a 1–0 lead into the ninth. Matty Alou pinch-hit to lead off the bottom of the frame and put down a perfect bunt that he beat out for a base hit. Terry did not lose his composure, demonstrating his mettle by striking out both Felipe Alou and Hiller, leaving the Giants just one out away from bitter defeat.

Terry faced a major problem at this point, when Willie Mays stepped to the plate. The Giants slugger promptly delivered a double to right field—but here's where many Giants fans lost their minds, as Alou failed to score from first. Upon further review, however, Maris, the Yankees' right fielder, fielded Mays' double and threw a strike to the cutoff man, second baseman Bobby Richardson, which likely would have led to Alou getting gunned down at the plate. Terry had gained a reprieve when Alou did not score, but he was hardly out of the woods as Willie McCovey and Orlando Cepeda—who had tallied 55 home runs between them during the 1962 season—were due up next.

The count went to 1–1 on McCovey, when Terry delivered a fastball. McCovey ripped into it with his mighty left-handed swing, sending a screaming line drive toward right field. Unfortunately for the Giants, though, the ball found Richardson as the Yankees' second baseman made a quick step to his left and raised his glove to snare the smash. In an instant, the Yankees were once again world champions, and the Giants felt as though this was the World Series that got away.

Charles Schulz, the creator of the beloved comic strip *Peanuts* and a Giants fan, expressed the frustration shared by all Giants fans in his December 22, 1962, strip: Charlie Brown and Linus look despondent for the first three panels before Charlie Brown laments, "Why couldn't McCovey have hit the ball just three feet higher?"

18 Mays Hits Four in One Game

On his 1966 comedy album, *Take-Offs and Put-Ons*, George Carlin performed a bit in which he was "Biff Burns" reading the sports. Reporting the fake news, he says, "In the sportlight spotlight tonight, first, a baseball trade: the San Francisco Giants today traded outfielder Willie Mays to the New York Mets in exchange for the entire Mets team. The Giants will also receive $500,000 in cash, two Eskimos, and a kangaroo."

While the routine was strictly comedy, there was a lot of truth behind the joke. Mays was considered the best player in baseball, and the Mets were the worst team by a landslide. At no time was the truth behind the joke more evident than during the game between the Giants and the Milwaukee Braves on April 30, 1961, at Milwaukee's County Stadium. Entering the contest, Mays felt anything but confidence about how he was swinging the bat. In the previous two games against the Braves, he had gone hitless in seven at-bats, prompting him to lament to reporters prior to the game that he was concerned about being in a slump.

Then the game began. Lou Burdette started for the Braves. Though he no longer dominated games as he once had, the veteran right-hander would go on to win 18 games in 1961. The April 30 game against the Giants would not be one of his wins. Chuck Hiller singled to lead off the first before Jim Davenport grounded into a double-play to bring Mays to the plate. One swing ended his slump as he connected for a 420-foot home run off Burdette to give the Giants a 1–0 lead.

Henry Aaron answered in the bottom half of the inning with a three-run homer off Giants starter Billy Loes. Mays then got his second turn at bat with two out in the third inning. Jose Pagan had opened the inning with a home run off Burdette, and Mays followed suit with a two-run homer that traveled 400 feet to put the Giants up 4–3. In the top of the fourth, Orlando Cepeda, Felipe Alou, and Pagan all homered to push the lead to 7–3. Moe Drabowsky retired Mays on a fly ball to center field in the fifth, but Mays got back on track in the sixth against Seth Morehead when he hit a 450-foot, three-run homer off the left-hander. In the eighth, Mays hit a 430-foot blast off Don McMahon to give him four home runs and eight RBIs on the day. When the Giants' half of the ninth came to a close, Mays was left standing in the on-deck circle when Davenport grounded out to end the inning, much to the chagrin of the Milwaukee crowd.

"I don't know what happened to me, but on my first time at bat today, I was seeing the ball better," Mays said. "When you hit two

The 15 Players Who've Hit Four HRs in a Game

Willie Mays became the ninth player in major league history to hit four home runs in one game when he did so on April 30, 1961. Here is the complete list of major leaguers who have hit four home runs in one game:

	Player	Date	Team	Opposing Team
1.	Bobby Lowe	May 30, 1894	Boston Beaneaters	Cincinnati Reds
2.	Ed Delahanty	July 13, 1896	Philadelphia Phillies	Chicago Colts
3.	Lou Gehrig	June 3, 1932	New York Yankees	Philadelphia A's
4.	Chuck Klein	July 10, 1936	Philadelphia Phillies	Pittsburgh Pirates
5.	Pat Seerey	July 18, 1948	Chicago White Sox	Philadelphia A's
6.	Gil Hodges	Aug. 31, 1950	Brooklyn Dodgers	Boston Braves
7.	Joe Adcock	July 31, 1954	Milwaukee Braves	Brooklyn Dodgers
8.	Rocky Colavito	June 10, 1959	Cleveland Indians	Baltimore Orioles
9.	Willie Mays	April 30, 1961	San Francisco Giants	Milwaukee Braves
10.	Mike Schmidt	April 17, 1976	Philadelphia Phillies	Chicago Cubs
11.	Bob Horner	July 6, 1986	Atlanta Braves	Montreal Expos
12.	Mark Whiten	Sept. 7, 1993	St. Louis Cardinals	Cincinnati Reds
13.	Mike Cameron	May 2, 2002	Seattle Mariners	Chicago White Sox
14.	Shawn Green	May 23, 2002	Los Angeles Dodgers	Milwaukee Brewers
15.	Carlos Delgado	Sept. 25, 2003	Toronto Blue Jays	Tampa Bay Devil Rays

homers in a game, that's something you don't expect anymore. Hitting four is hard to believe."

Mays had been the centerpiece of the Giants' 14-run attack that afternoon. During the course of the game, the Giants hit eight home runs, bringing them to a total of 13 for two games; both tied major league records. Aaron hit two home runs, making for 10 in the game, which also tied a National League mark for one game. By hitting four home runs in one game, Mays became only the ninth player in major league history at the time to turn the trick.

"When I'm not hitting, I don't hit nobody," Mays said. "But, when I'm hitting, I hit anybody." Mays called the game his greatest day in baseball. "I was just up there swinging," he said.

19 Bobby Bonds

Bobby Bonds brought a different kind of athlete to the major leagues when he arrived with the Giants in 1968. Not only could Bonds hit for power, he could run like an Olympic sprinter, which was little wonder, given the gene pool from which he came. Bonds had a sister who participated in the 1964 Olympics in Tokyo as a sprinter and a brother who was accomplished enough in football to be selected in the NFL Draft.

Bobby could hold his own, being named a high school All-American in track and field, in addition to being honored as the Southern California High School Athlete of the Year in 1964. On August 4, 1964, Bonds signed with the Giants. Almost four years later, he would make his major league debut on June 25, 1968. And what a glorious debut. Bonds hit a grand slam in his first game. Only five players in major league history have turned the trick to date, and he was just the second to do so—the list includes Bill Duggleby (1898), Jeremy Hermida (2005), Kevin Kouzmanoff (2006), and Daniel Nava (2010).

Bonds finished his rookie season with nine home runs in 81 games. The following season he jumped to 32 home runs with 90 RBIs and 45 stolen bases. Bonds hit 20-plus home runs and at least 70 RBIs the next five seasons. But along with the good came the bad, which meant strikeouts, a lot of strikeouts for Bonds. Many times when Bonds whipped his bat through the strike zone, he came away with only air. In 1969 he set a major league record with 187 strikeouts. But his performance would make baseball purists question if striking out really was as bad as perceived since he also managed to score a National League–leading 120 runs in 1969. In

1970 Bonds pushed his strikeout record to 189, and that record would stand until Adam Dunn struck out 195 times in 2004.

Still, Bonds brought such a unique look to baseball that nobody really knew what to make of him. In 1973 he hit 39 home runs and stole 43 bases, coming the closest of anyone to founding the 40-40 club until 1988, when Jose Canseco finally managed to do it with 42 homers and 40 stolen bases. While playing for the Giants, he won the three Gold Gloves and made the National League All-Star team twice, including the 1973 midsummer classic in which he earned Most Valuable Player honors. The Giants traded

Bobby Bonds takes a cut during a game in 1969. He played for San Francisco from 1968 to 1974 and came a home run away from founding the 40-40 club in 1973, 23 years before his son would become a member with the Giants.

Bonds to the New York Yankees for Bobby Murcer following the 1974 season. All told, Bonds spent seven seasons with the Giants, hitting .273 with 186 home runs, 552 RBIs, 263 stolen bases, and 1,016 strikeouts.

Bonds became well-traveled after leaving the Giants. After playing one season for the Yankees, he finished his 14-year major league career in stints with the California Angels, Chicago White Sox, Texas Rangers, Cleveland Indians, St. Louis Cardinals, and Chicago Cubs. Bonds finished his career with 332 home runs and 461 stolen bases, making him the only player other than his son, Barry, to hit 300 home runs and steal 400 bases.

Bobby Bonds died of cancer on August 23, 2003.

20 Watch M*A*S*H Episode No. 204

One of the most popular shows in TV history was *M*A*S*H*, which aired on CBS beginning on September 17, 1972, and ran until February 28, 1983. The series was adapted from the 1970 movie *M*A*S*H*, which stared Donald Sutherland and Elliott Gould and depicted life at the 4077th Mobile Army Surgical Hospital in South Korea during the Korean War. While the movie was good, the characters from the TV series—such as Hawkeye Pierce, B.J. Honeycutt, Frank Burns, Margaret Houlihan, and Colonel Sherman Potter—live on in syndication.

So what the heck does *M*A*S*H* have to do with Giants fans? It's all about episode No. 204 of the ninth season, which first aired on December 29, 1980. Giants fans who have seen it will never forget it; and if you're a Giants fans who hasn't seen it, you need to.

The episode begins on New Year's Day 1951, and from there the year is reviewed in different scenes. Along the way, Father

Mulcahy grows a garden, the doctors work to create an artificial kidney machine, and Margaret begins to knit as a hobby. But of most interest to any Giants fan worth his or her immaculate 1954 Willie Mays Topps baseball card is the developing story between Major Charles Winchester and Corporal Max Klinger. Winchester comes from an aristocratic New England family while Klinger hails from the other side of the tracks in Toledo, Ohio. In March Klinger is seen wearing a baseball glove while talking up the Brooklyn Dodgers to Potter, which leads to a $20 bet between the two. Klinger takes the Dodgers to win the National League pennant, while Potter takes the St. Louis Cardinals.

While the other story lines develop, the Dodgers take a nine-game lead over the rest of the National League, prompting Klinger to get cocky, running his mouth and offering a new bet: the Dodgers against the entire National League for 2-to-1 odds. Potter decides to take him up on the bet and wants to let $50 ride on the outcome. Klinger decides the bet has grown too rich and opts to rescind his offer. That's when Winchester steps in. Though his character is opposed to anything as pedestrian as baseball, Winchester likes the odds of the Dodgers against the rest of the National League and offers to back Klinger.

The Dodgers continue to increase their lead, further sucking in Winchester, who raises the stakes to 6-to-1 to get more action. Shortly thereafter, the Dodgers begin a nose dive while the Giants begin to make their ascent to the top of the league. All the while, Winchester begins to dog Klinger for his instituting the bet in the first place. By the end of the season, as the Dodgers' lead has dwindled to nothing, Klinger is seen hiding from Winchester, who has begun to take every Dodgers loss as if a death in the family had occurred. When the final game of the season is played in the playoff between the Giants and the Dodgers, the entire camp is tuned into the broadcast. Winchester is wearing a Dodgers hat and listening to the ballgame like the average fan—which normally would have been far below his standing. Then Bobby Thomson connects, and throughout the camp, Russ Hodges' voice is yelling over the radio, "The Giants win the pennant!"

The parting shot from that scene shows Winchester and Klinger after each has fainted. At the end of the episode, the entire camp is watching a newsreel from 1951 as it is shown via a projector against a bedsheet. When Thomson's dramatic home run is shown, Winchester bursts through, shredding the sheet with a knife. In other words, can't-miss joy for any Giants fan.

Giants MVPs

Almost from the beginning of the major leagues, there has been an award to recognize the most valuable player in the league. From 1911 to 1914, it was called the Chalmers Award, which officially recognized the player who contributed the most to his team's success. Second baseman Larry Doyle took home the honor in 1912, the only Giant to win it. Next came the League Award from 1922 to 1929. No Giant won this award. No official honor was awarded in 1930, but after that came the Most Valuable Player award. The Baseball Writers Association of America (BBWAA) has presented it every fall since 1931, and it is considered the official MVP award, even though a host of other awards have sprung up since.

Carl Hubbell became the first Giant to win an MVP, which he did in 1933 after "King Carl" went 23–12 with a 1.66 ERA. Included in his MVP season were 22 complete games and 10 shutouts. He won it again in 1936 when he went 26–6 with a 2.31 ERA.

Willie Mays also won the award twice. He first was recognized as the MVP in 1954 after hitting .345 with 41 home runs and 110 RBIs. Mays claimed his second MVP award in 1965 for a season that saw him hit 52 home runs with 112 RBIs while hitting .317. The "Say Hey Kid" also finished second in the balloting in 1958 and 1962.

Willie McCovey claimed his first and only MVP in 1969 when he had his best season in the major leagues. "Stretch" hit .320 with 45 home runs and 126 RBIs that season.

Barry Bonds joined the Giants in 1993 as a high-priced free agent, and the Giants' investment began to show a yield in Bonds' first season with the team when he hit .336 with 46 home runs and 123 RBIs and was named the National League's Most Valuable Player. Miraculously, eight years after winning his first award with the Giants (he won two with the Pirates), Bonds won his second in 2001, a season that saw the slugger set the single-season home run record with 73. Winning the award in 2001 would begin a run of four consecutive seasons (2001–2004) in which Bonds would be honored as the league's MVP. During that period, Bonds hit 209 home runs and led the Giants to the World Series in 2002, where they would lose to the Angels in seven games. Bonds also finished second in the MVP balloting in 2000.

Two other Giants players also won the MVP award: Kevin Mitchell, who came to the Giants from the San Diego Padres, won the award in his third season with the Giants in 1989 after hitting .291 with 47 home runs and 125 RBIs. That would serve as the high-water mark for the barrel-chested outfielder from San Diego. A well-traveled second baseman found his game with the Giants, and he would win the MVP award in 2000. Preceding Bonds' four consecutive wins, Jeff Kent's MVP year began a streak of five straight MVP awards for San Francisco. Kent, who had played for the Toronto Blue Jays, New York Mets, and Cleveland Indians prior to joining the Giants, came into his prime while playing in San Francisco. Kent spent six seasons with the Giants and had his best season in 2000 when he hit .334 while hitting 33 home runs and driving in 125.

Fans watch Game 2 of the 1905 World Series between the Philadelphia Athletics and the New York Giants from Coogan's Bluff, overlooking the Polo Grounds in Manhattan, on October 10.

22 First World Series

Imagine getting into the World Series and deciding not to go. Sounds crazy, but it happened in 1904 when the Giants, under the direction of John McGraw, opted to take a pass. Why? Simple explanation, actually. McGraw did not feel that a team from the new—and inferior, in his view—American League was worthy of playing the champions from the National League. In the great McGraw's mind, the American League was a glorified minor league.

Initially, McGraw felt that the New York Highlanders were a lock to win the American League, which made the prospect of participating in the World Series even less appealing. To McGraw's way of thinking, playing a team from the same city—that competed for the same customers—and a team he deemed of lesser quality meant his Giants would have nothing to gain by beating them, yet they would have everything to lose if they were to fall to the Highlanders. In addition, McGraw had some bad blood with the Highlanders from his two seasons managing the team when they were the Baltimore Orioles.

McGraw and the Giants were dealt a surprise, however, when the Highlanders lost to the Boston Americans on the final day of the season to lose their place in the World Series. Nevertheless, the Giants manager stuck to his guns, which translated to the Giants following through with their boycott.

A year later, in 1905, the Little Napoleon would relent, and the Giants would play in their first World Series—and what a remarkable exhibition of baseball that World Series turned out to be. The Giants' opponent was the Philadelphia Athletics, and the Series was changed from the best-of-nine-games format of the 1903 World Series to a best-of-seven format.

The first game took place at Philadelphia's Columbia Park and saw a pitching duel unfold between Christy Mathewson of the Giants and Eddie Plank of the Athletics. Clearly in his prime, Mathewson pitched a complete game shutout as the Giants took the first game 3–0. The series shifted to the Polo Grounds in New York for Game 2 and saw another stellar pitching matchup between Chief Bender for the Athletics and Joe McGinnity for the Giants. Bender handcuffed the Giants all day, and the Athletics supported him with three unearned runs as the Athletics evened the series with a 3–0 win. Game 3 was played in Philadelphia and went to the Giants 9–0 as Mathewson pitched his second shutout to move the Giants to within two games of clinching the Series.

Games 4 and 5 took place at the Polo Grounds, and the Giants won both by respective scores of 1–0 and 2–0, with Mathewson besting Bender by pitching the third of his three complete game shutouts in Game 5 to make the Giants world champions.

Though the World Series was in its infancy, some remarkable accomplishments took place in the five games. For starters, each game was won by a complete game shutout. And even though the Giants lost one game, they did not allow an earned run during the World Series, which translated to the Giants finishing the set with a 0.00 ERA, a record that can only be tied but never broken. Though the Giants would play in the World Series four times between 1905 and 1920, they would not win another Fall Classic until 1921.

All Alou

The odds of getting to the major leagues are astronomical. In the 1960s those odds were particularly great when considering the population, the limited number of teams in the major leagues, and the fact that baseball ranked as the most popular sport. So consider the incredible achievement carved out by the three Alou brothers, who not only reached the major leagues but also played for the same team and at the same time.

Felipe Alou played the outfield and made his major league debut in 1958, becoming an All-Star in 1962 when he batted .316 with 25 home runs and 98 RBIs. When he joined the Giants, he became the first native of the Dominican Republic to reach the major leagues. A long list of his countrymen would follow, including brothers Matty and Jesus. Matty joined the Giants in 1960, and Jesus joined his brothers with the Giants in 1963, setting up what would be a unique situation.

On September 10, 1963, the Giants were playing the New York Mets at the Polo Grounds. Felipe started the game in right field and led off with a crowd of 14,945 watching. In the top of the eighth, with the Giants trailing 3–0, Giants manager Alvin Dark inserted

Jesus into the game as a pinch-hitter for Jose Pagan, and he grounded out against right-hander Carl Willey for the first out. Matty then pinch hit for pitcher Bob Garibaldi and struck out for the second out, only to bring up the third of the brothers, Felipe, who grounded out to end the inning. While the Alou brothers had made all three outs in the inning, they had become the first trio of brothers to play as teammates in a major league game.

Because the Giants had outfielders Willie Mays and Willie McCovey, who also played first base, the prospect of getting the three brothers into the same outfield during the same game seemed remote. But in a September 15 game against the Pirates at Pittsburgh's Forbes Field, Felipe Alou started in right field with Mays starting in center and McCovey in left. The Giants scored three in the first before the Pirates came back with one in the fourth and two in the fifth to tie the game. But after the Giants scored five in the seventh, Jesus entered the game and went to right field, prompting Felipe to move to left. The Giants then scored four runs in the eighth to take a 12–3 lead. That's when Dark decided to make the historic change.

In the bottom of the eighth, Matty entered the game in left field in Mays' spot, and Felipe moved to center field. Suddenly the Giants had an all-Alou outfield. The Giants won the game 13–5, and what the 18,916 fans saw that day was a first in major league history: three brothers had never before played together in the same outfield. They would all play the outfield together for one more game before the end of the 1963 season.

Prior to the 1964 season, Felipe was traded to the Braves, where he would flourish as a player, which eliminated the possibility of having an all-Alou outfield again. Matty and Jesus would later find their way to other teams, each of them carving out decent major league careers. By the time all of the brothers had retired, they had played in 5,129 games and collected more hits than any other trio of brothers in major league history.

24 Carl Hubbell's 1934 All-Star Game

"King Carl" dazzled throughout his Hall of Fame career, but Carl Hubbell never looked better than he did during the 1934 All-Star Game. On July 10, 1934, the second-ever All-Star Game took place at the Polo Grounds, and Hubbell got the starting nod at his home park with 48,368 watching.

While the game was an exhibition, league pride was at stake, and Hubbell wanted to do well in front of the home crowd. Initially the chances of Hubbell having any semblance of a good outing looked remote. Charlie Gehringer singled to lead off the game and went to second on an outfield error. Hubbell then issued a walk to Heinie Manush, which wasn't exactly what the left-hander had in mind with the likes of Babe Ruth, Lou Gehrig, and Jimmie Foxx to follow. A conference on the mound ensued, in which Travis Jackson, Pie Traynor, Bill Terry, and Frankie Frisch congregated to determine if Hubbell was going to be all right. After the meeting broke up, Hubbell stared in at Ruth standing in the batter's box.

Hubbell first wasted a fastball, then delivered three straight screwballs, all for strikes. Ruth stared at home plate umpire Cy Pfirman, then walked back to the visiting dugout while Gehrig moved to the plate. Hoping to get Gehrig to roll over one of his screwballs so he could get a double play, Hubbell threw four pitches to the Iron Horse, with the fourth being a screwball that Gehrig swung at for strike three to evoke a roar from the crowd.

Foxx was up next, and Gehringer and Manush executed a double steal with the Athletics' slugger at the plate. Hubbell wasn't rattled in the least as he looked in for the signal from catcher Gabby Hartnett. The Cubs' catcher signaled for a screwball, and

Foxx struck out swinging after looking at a succession of screwballs. Hubbell had thrown 12 pitches and retired the side on three strikeouts.

Frisch homered in the bottom of the first to give the National League a 1–0 lead. Hubbell then returned to the mound to face Al Simmons. Simmons struck out, and Joe Cronin followed by striking out, giving Hubbell five consecutive strikeouts of five future Hall of Fame players.

Bill Dickey finally broke Hubbell's spell with a two-out single before Hubbell finished off the second by striking out pitcher Lefty Gomez. Hubbell returned to the mound in the third and retired Gehringer on a fly-out to right field and Manush on a ground-out

1933 Another World Championship

Bill Terry took over as manager of the Giants during the 1932 season when iconic manager John McGraw stepped down from his post. In Terry's second campaign in 1933, the Giants returned to the World Series after capturing the National League pennant with a 91–61 record. The Giants' opponent in the series was the Washington Senators.

Terry successfully navigated his pitching staff, led by Carl Hubbell and Hal Schumacher, throughout the season, as the two aces combined for 42 wins. The pair would be just as dominating during the World Series. With Hubbell leading the way, the Giants took Game 1 by the score of 4–2 behind a complete game five-hitter by Hubbell. Schumacher followed suit in the second game with a complete game five-hitter in a 6–1 Giants win.

Washington came back in Game 3, winning 4–0, before the tandem of Hubbell and Schumacher returned for seconds. Hubbell started Game 4 and allowed no earned runs in a complete game, 11-inning, 2–1 Giants victory to move to within one game of capturing the Series. Schumacher then surrendered three runs in 5⅔ innings in Game 5, but Dolf Luque effectively closed the door by throwing 4⅓ innings of scoreless relief as the Giants took a 4–3 win in 10 innings to nab their first championship since 1922, their fourth overall. Not since the 1933 World Series has a World Series game been played in the nation's capital. The Giants would not win another World Series until 1954, when they defeated the Cleveland Indians.

to second. After walking Ruth, Hubbell retired the last batter he faced, Gehrig, on a fly-out to right field.

Hubbell's final line read: no runs on two hits, two bases on balls, and six strikeouts in just three innings pitched. While the Giants left-hander performed brilliantly, he did not get the win. The American League scored six runs in the fifth inning en route to a 9–7 win with Cleveland's Mel Harder getting credit for the win. While the American League won the game, few remember that fact. What marked the second annual midsummer classic was the performance by King Carl.

25 Make a Trip to Cooperstown

A must for any true Giants fans is a trip to the National Baseball Hall of Fame and Museum in Cooperstown, New York. Enshrined on the hallowed baseball grounds are 61 players, managers, and executives with ties to the New York/San Francisco Giants organization. Of that number, 25 spent the majority of their careers with the Giants. Notables among them include Bill Terry, Gaylord Perry, Buck Ewing, Orlando Cepeda, Juan Marichal, Christy Mathewson, John McGraw, and Willie Mays.

The Hall of Fame is open every day except Thanksgiving, Christmas, and New Year's Day from 9:00 AM to 5:00 PM. A great idea is to combine a visit to the Hall with a Giants East Coast road trip—whether they are playing in Philadelphia, Boston, or New York, it's within reasonable driving distance.

Of course, there are the many individual plaques and miscellaneous artifacts for the different Giants Hall of Famers, along with video highlights of their many accomplishments. Aside from those tributes, some other interesting items at the Hall of Fame that would interest Giants fans include the following:

- Catcher's gear used by Bengie Molina in 2009
- Cap worn by Jonathan Sanchez and a baseball from his no-hitter on July 10, 2009, the 13th in Giants history
- Cap worn by Randy Johnson during his 300th career win on June 4, 2009, and a baseball and the Nationals Park pitching rubber from the game
- Jersey from Tim Lincecum's Cy Young–winning 2008 season
- Ball signed on May 16, 2008, by Masanori Murakami, the first Japanese-born player in MLB history, who debuted in 1964
- Cap and spikes worn by Omar Vizquel when he broke Luis Aparicio's record for most games played at shortstop on May 25, 2008
- Barry Bonds' record-breaking 756th career home run ball from August 7, 2007, which was branded with an asterisk
- Helmets from Barry Bonds' record-tying 755th and record-breaking 756th home runs on August 4 and 7, 2007
- Balls signed by the Giants lineup and by umpires from the August 7, 2007, game when Barry Bonds hit home run No. 756
- Jersey worn by Omar Vizquel when he turned his MLB record 1,591st double play on May 13, 2007
- Lineup card and final out ball from 10,000th win in franchise history, a 4–3 victory over the Dodgers on July 14, 2005
- Jersey with "Gigantes" on the front, worn by manager Felipe Alou during Spanish jersey weekend on May 21–22, 2005
- Jersey worn by Jason Schmidt to record his 251st strikeout, October 3, 2004, setting the Giants' single-season record

- Bat used by Barry Bonds to hit the longest home run in AT&T Park history on June 7, 2001
- Bat used by Rich Aurilia to hit the first grand slam in interleague play on June 14, 1997
- Bat used by Willie McCovey on August 25, 1979, to hit his 520th career home run
- Ball from John Monetefusco's no-hit game on September 29, 1976
- Ball from Gaylord Perry's no-hitter on September 17, 1968
- Ball that Mel Ott hit for his 500th career home run on August 1, 1945
- Giants sweater worn by Billy Terry
- Jersey worn by Travis Jackson
- Player contract from 1899 signed Christy Mathewson

Easy Giants Trivia

Questions
1. Who was the "Say Hey Kid"?
2. Willie Mays hit more than 700 home runs, true or false?
3. Who was the "Dominican Dandy"?
4. What team did the Giants defeat in the 1954 World Series?
5. What player's nickname was "Stretch"?
6. What was the name of the field where the Giants played their games before moving from New York to San Francisco?
7. What Giants slugger holds the single-season home run record?
8. What Hall of Famer had the nickname "Cha-Cha"?
9. What was the name of the ballpark originally built for the Giants when they moved to San Francisco?
10. Who threw the Giants' first no-hitter once the team became the San Francsico Giants?

Answers

1. Willie Mays; 2. False; 3. Juan Marichal; 4. Cleveland Indians; 5. Willie McCovey; 6. The Polo Grounds; 7. Barry Bonds; 8. Orlando Cepeda; 9. Candlestick Park; 10. Juan Marichal

26 John Roseboro Incident

Over the years, descriptions of bloodshed and battles between two teams that despised one another chronicled the games played between the Giants and the Los Angeles Dodgers. On August 22, 1965, the action did not need to be hyped, as actual blood was spilled when the two teams met at Candlestick Park.

A classic pitching duel between Juan Marichal and Sandy Koufax was set to take place that Sunday afternoon, but the game assumed a combative flavor rather than a competitive one from the outset. The Dodgers led 2–1 by the time Marichal stepped to the plate in the third inning. Given the fact that Marichal had already dusted Maury Wills and Ron Fairly with brushback pitches, John Roseboro wanted to send Marichal a message. Initially, the Dodgers catcher wanted Koufax to do the deed by drilling Marichal, but Koufax wanted no part of such an action. So Roseboro took matters into his own hands.

Once Roseboro caught one of Koufax's pitches, Roseboro's return throw to Koufax nearly grazed Marichal's nose. Roseboro stood a solid 5'11", 190 pounds, and had studied karate, so he figured he would mop the diamond with Marichal if he took exception to any of his antics. Roseboro's first throw caught Marichal's attention, the next throw, which nearly clipped one of Marichal's ears, triggered an avalanche of emotions from the Giants right-hander. It turned out that Roseboro's karate training was no match for a baseball bat. Marichal proceeded to strike Roseboro on the head three times with his bat. The blows created a two-inch gash on Roseboro's head—which would require 14 stitches—and sent blood everywhere while setting off a bench-clearing brawl.

For 14 minutes both teams went after one another in a fashion uncharacteristic of most baseball fights. In other words, the combatants weren't going through the motions, they actually wanted to bring harm to the other team during the fight. Finally, order was restored, thanks in large part to the peacemaking efforts of Koufax and Willie Mays.

In the aftermath of the brawl, Marichal was ejected from the game and received a nine-game suspension from National League president Warren Giles, along with a fine of $1,750. Included in his punishment was a mandate that he could not attend the Giants' final series of the season in Los Angeles against the Dodgers. Many felt Marichal's punishment was not stiff enough since he would miss just two starts, but his real punishment was served for years after the incident, as Marichal's image suffered irreparable damage. Photographs from the fight found sports pages from coast to coast the following day, in addition to the cover of *Life* magazine, and Marichal, who hailed from the Dominican Republic, was characterized as the stereotyped hot-headed Latin.

Roseboro brought a civil suit against Marichal that was settled out of court, and later the pair formed an unlikely friendship. Years after Marichal retired, the Giants right-hander—who had undeniable Hall of Fame credentials—was not elected to the Hall of Fame for the simple reason many baseball writers still held the incident against him.

Roseboro ended up speaking on Marichal's behalf, telling everyone that Marichal had not been responsible for the fight, he had been, and Marichal eventually was elected to the Hall of Fame in 1983 and thanked Roseboro during his induction speech. Marichal and Roseboro managed to put the fight so far behind them that they would later autograph photographs of the incident. Roseboro died on August 16, 2002, and Marichal spoke at the funeral.

Will Clark

"Will the Thrill" came to the Giants with the second overall pick in the 1985 Major League Baseball Draft. One year later, Will Clark was at first base for the Giants.

Clark won the Golden Spikes Award and became an All-American while playing for Mississippi State University, where he was a teammate of Rafael Palmeiro's. Together they became one of the most formidable hitting tandems college baseball had ever known.

Though Clark possessed a slender build, he had the sweetest of swings, which prompted baseball players from Little League to the major leagues to try and emulate the same action. Giants fans eagerly awaited Clark's arrival to the major leagues and weren't disappointed when he finally arrived to make his debut as the Giants first baseman on April 8, 1986, at the age of 22. Not only did Clark homer in his first at-bat, he did so against future Hall of Fame pitcher Nolan Ryan in a game against the Astros in the Astrodome. Clark also hit a home run in the first game he played at Candlestick Park. Although Clark's rookie season was cut short by an elbow injury, he finished with a .287 average that included 11 home runs and 41 RBIs.

Following his abbreviated rookie campaign, Clark became a fixture at first base for the Giants. In 1987 he hit .308 with 91 RBIs and a career-high 35 home runs. The following season, he became the National League's starting first baseman for the All-Star Game, and he would get voted in as a starter every year from 1988 through 1992.

Will Clark smashes one of his two home runs off of Chicago starting pitcher Greg Maddux during Game 1 of the NLCS versus the Cubs at Wrigley Field on October 4, 1989. Photo courtesy of AP Images

Given the weather constraints put on hitters at Candlestick Park, offensive numbers were often hard to accrue while playing for the Giants. But Clark overcame the weather and became the first Giants player since Bobby Murcer (1975–1976) to have consecutive seasons with 90-plus RBIs. From 1987 through 1991, Clark had at least 90 RBIs every season, establishing a career high of 116 in 1991. Clark finished second in the National League in hitting in 1989, which was his best season with the Giants, as he hit .333 with 23 home runs and 111 RBIs to help lead the Giants to the postseason.

Clark's excellence rang true throughout his body of work with the Giants, but at no time did he shine brighter than he did during the 1989 National League Championship Series when the Giants defeated the Cubs to advance to the World Series. In Game 1, Clark hit two home runs off Cubs starter Greg Maddux, including a grand slam. Then, in the deciding Game 5, Clark had a two-run single in the bottom of the eighth that broke a 1–1 tie and led the Giants to their first World Series since 1962.

Clark was voted the NLCS MVP after hitting .650 with two home runs and eight RBIs. He then struggled in the World Series against the Oakland Athletics, when he did not drive in a run and the Giants were swept in four games.

His production began to wane in the 1992 and 1993 seasons, which kept the Giants from offering him a long-term contract once he became a free agent prior to the 1994 season. Ironically, Clark signed with the Texas Rangers to replace Palmeiro at first base. He would enjoy some good years with the Rangers, but nothing compared to his production while he was with the Giants. In eight seasons with the Giants, Clark hit .299 with 176 home runs and 709 RBIs. After playing with Texas for five seasons, he finished his career with stints in Baltimore and St. Louis.

28 Memorable Marichal-Spahn Matchup

Juan Marichal had some memorable performances during his illustrious 16-year career, which included a no-hitter. But none of those performances could hold a candle to his outing on July 2, 1963. The Giants hosted the Milwaukee Braves at Candlestick Park, as 15,921 watched the Tuesday evening affair with great interest because the upstart Giants right-hander faced veteran left-hander Warren Spahn.

Spahn, at the age of 42, carried an 11–3 mark to the mound for the Braves, who were 38–38 on the season. Marichal entered the game at the age of 25 with a 12–3 record, which had helped fuel a 44–34 record for the Giants. Three weeks prior to Marichal's start, he had thrown a no-hitter against the Houston Colt .45s on June 15 that came up two walks short of a perfect game. And he had been on the losing end of a no-hitter to Sandy Koufax on May 11.

Neither Marichal nor Spahn would have the day off, considering the lineups they faced. Marichal would see future Hall of Famers Hank Aaron and Eddie Mathews in the Braves' lineup, while Spahn would see future Hall of Famers Willie McCovey, Willie Mays, and Orlando Cepeda. The two pitchers' performances that day would help explain why each would also become enshrined at Cooperstown.

Soon the goose eggs began to nest on the scoreboard. McCovey hit a ball in the ninth that appeared to clear the foul pole in right, which would have ended the game. Chris Pelekoudas, the first-base umpire, viewed the drive differently and called it foul. McCovey then grounded out to first base for the second out of the inning.

After nine innings, the game remained deadlocked in a scoreless tie. Though the era was not known for coddling pitchers, Marichal had to plead his case to Alvin Dark about remaining in the game, and the Giants manager allowed him to do so. Dark's decision began to lose some of its conviction in the 13th inning when the game remained scoreless. When the game reached the 14th, Dark finally had seen enough when he told Marichal he was taking him out of the game. Marichal would not give in, as he recounted to the *New York Times* what he told Dark: "I said, 'Do you see that man on the mound?' and I was pointing at Warren. 'That man is 42, and I'm 25. I'm not ready for you to take me out.'"

In the top of the 16th inning, Marichal retired Frank Bolling and Aaron on fly-outs to right and center fields before surrendering a single to Denis Menke. He ended the inning by getting Norm Larker to ground back to the mound. Harvey Kuenn flew out to start the bottom of the 16th to bring Mays to the plate. Spahn

Longest Games in Giants History

If you're one of those fans who can't get enough of Giants baseball, you would have been in hog heaven on May 29, 2001, when the Giants played the Arizona Diamondbacks. That contest would turn out to be the longest in the history of AT&T Park. Armando Reynoso started for the Diamondbacks; Shawn Estes started for the Giants; and what followed were goose eggs, a lot of goose eggs. Reynoso threw six scoreless innings, and Estes tossed seven scoreless before each left the game. A total of 12 additional pitchers followed in the game, as the zeroes continued to mount on the scoreboard. Through 17 innings, the game stood deadlocked in a 0–0 tie.

In the top of the 18th, D'backs center fielder Steve Finley drew a one-out walk, and backup first baseman Erubiel Durazo followed with a double to left off Ryan Vogelsong, driving home Finley and giving Arizona a 1–0 lead. With the bench depleted, Vogelsong had to hit for himself leading off the bottom of the 18th, and he doubled to left-center field. He would advance to third on a ground-out, but that is where he was stranded, as the Diamondbacks preserved a 1–0 win in a game that took five hours, 53 minutes to play.

While that was a long day, what happened on May 31, 1964, made the longest home contest feel like a quick game of pepper. The Giants played a doubleheader at Shea Stadium that day and took the first game 5–3 in two hours, 29 minutes, before taking the field for the second game. What followed was lengthy. Through nine innings, the score was tied at 6—then 13 scoreless innings followed. In the top of the 23rd inning, Del Crandall had an RBI double, and Jesus Alou followed with an RBI single to give the Giants an 8–6 lead. Bob Hendley retired the side in the bottom half of the inning, and the Giants won the second game—in seven hours, 23 minutes. Which means anyone who stayed for the entirety of both games saw just about 10 hours of baseball. Who says you can't have too much of a good thing?

wound and delivered. Mays swung at Spahn's first pitch and rerouted a screwball—which Spahn said "didn't break worth a damn"—over the left-field wall to give the Giants a 1–0 win and Marichal a well-deserved decision.

For his evening, Marichal allowed no runs on eight hits while walking four and striking out 10 in 16 innings. Meanwhile, Spahn allowed one run on nine hits with a walk and two strikeouts in 15⅓ innings. Amazingly the game lasted just four hours and 10 minutes.

Sadly, Spahn had experienced the losing end of a similar marathon in the past when he lost to Brooklyn in 1951 with two outs in the 16th inning, and when he lost to the Cubs in 1952 in 15 innings after striking out 18.

In 1966 Marichal would win another lengthy contest when he beat the Philadelphia Phillies 1–0 in 14 innings. But he found himself on the losing side in 1969 when Tommie Agee of the New York Mets homered with one out in the 14th to beat him 1–0.

29 Giants Move to San Francisco

The 1954 season championship season served as the Giants' high-water mark for the 1950s. In 1955 the team finished third, and support for the team began to deteriorate, as did the Polo Grounds, the aged stadium where they played. In 1956 attendance fell to 629,179 while the Giants sought a new venue to call home. When a solution could not be found in the New York City area, Giants majority owner Horace Stoneham began to consider other alternatives, such as relocating the team to another city eager to support a major league team.

Initially, the Minneapolis–St. Paul area appeared to be the preferred destination for the club. Metropolitan Stadium was in place and housed the Giants' top minor league team, the Minneapolis Millers. Based on the fact the Giants owned the Millers, they had the rights to put a team in Minneapolis.

But another option presented itself when Stoneham met with San Francisco mayor George Christopher, who offered the Giants' owner a municipal stadium with 12,000 parking spaces. No major league teams were located west of Missouri at the time, which made the prospect of relocating to California seem about as remote as travel to the moon. However, at the same time, the Brooklyn Dodgers were in negotiations with the City of Los Angeles. But due to the prospect of being an isolated major league team in California, Dodgers owner Walter O'Malley had been informed that they would not be allowed to move unless a second team went to California as well. Thus Stoneham had Mayor Christopher as well as O'Malley in his ear, touting the merits of heading to the Golden State.

Eventually, Stoneham—with the Giants in the midst of another dismal year of attendance at the Polo Grounds—and O'Malley were convinced that moving west would be the wisest move for them to make, prompting the Giants and Dodgers to announce during the 1957 season that they intended to relocate to San Francisco and Los Angeles, respectively, for the 1958 season.

A crowd of 11,606 showed up at the Polo Grounds for the Giants' final game in New York on September 29, 1957. The Pirates defeated the Giants 9–1 to give the Giants a 69–85 record and a sixth-place finish for the 1957 season. Stoneham spoke to noted author Roger Angell about the final game when he said: "The last day we played there, I couldn't go to the game. I just didn't want to see it come to an end."

The San Francisco Seals of the Pacific Coast League were the only professional baseball team in San Francisco, as they had played in the city since 1903. Because of the Giants' relocation, the Seals were forced to leave San Francisco. The team moved to Phoenix prior to the 1958 season and became an affiliate of the Giants. The Seals' home ballpark, Seals Stadium, became the new home of the Giants, who played in the historic minor league park in 1958 and 1959 before Candlestick Park opened for play in 1960.

On April 15, 1958, the San Francisco Giants beat the Los Angeles Dodgers 8–0 at Seals Stadium in the first major league

Candlestick Park as it looked when it opened in 1960. It would remain the Giants' often-frigid home ballpark in San Francisco up until 1999.

game on the West Coast. In two years of play at Seals Stadium, the Giants attracted over 2 million fans before Candlestick Park opened in 1960, which essentially completed the Giants' move to San Francisco. The Giants played their final game at Seals Stadium on September 20, 1959, when 22,923 watched the Dodgers defeat the Giants 8–2.

Horace Stoneham

Horace Stoneham served as the owner of the Giants for 40 years. He became an executive with the Giants when his father, Charles Stoneham, owned and operated the team. When his father died in 1936, Horace became the primary owner of the Giants at the age of 32. During Horace's first two years as the owner he experienced great success, as the Giants won the National League pennant in consecutive seasons.

Among the brassier moves Stoneham made was the hiring of Leo Durocher in 1948. What made the move interesting, and somewhat cheeky, was the fact Durocher managed the Brooklyn Dodgers at the time; in addition, he always seemed to be in trouble stemming from myriad vices. But the move turned out to be a good one, as the club again reached prominence with Durocher at the helm, claiming National League pennants in 1951 and 1954 and winning the World Series in 1954.

However, the Durocher move paled when compared to the boldest move he made when he moved the Giants to San Francisco in 1958, accompanying the Brooklyn Dodgers to the Golden State. Under Stoneham, the Giants won the National League pennant once again in 1962 before the club experienced a major attendance drop, which prompted him to make a failed attempt to sell the team to an ownership group that would have moved the team to Toronto. Eventually, the club was sold in 1976 to Bob Lurie. Stoneham died in 1990.

30 Dave Dravecky

Dave Dravecky came to the Giants on July 5, 1987, when the Giants traded pitchers Mark Grant, Keith Comstock, and Mark Davis, along with third baseman Chris Brown, to the Padres for Dravecky, pitcher Craig Lefferts, and third baseman Kevin Mitchell. By that point in the time, Dravecky had already been a National League All-Star and had pitched in the World Series when the Padres lost to the Tigers in the 1984 Fall Classic. The left-hander had a career ERA of 3.12 in his six seasons with the Padres, where he had been used as a starter and reliever. Though hardly overpowering, Dravecky knew how to pitch, and at the age of 31, he appeared to have his best years ahead of him when he moved to San Francisco, where he became a full-time starter.

Making 18 starts for the Giants in the second half of the 1987 season, he went 7–5 with a 3.20 ERA to help the Giants win the National League West division, which earned the team a spot in the National League Championship Series against the St. Louis Cardinals. Dravecky got the starting nod in Game 2 of the NLCS and pitched a complete game shutout. He returned to start Game 6, but took the loss as the Cardinals edged the Giants 1–0. The Cardinals then won Game 7 to advance to the World Series.

Dravecky came away from the playoffs looking like one of the top starters in baseball, fueling the hopes of Giants fans that they had a marquee pitcher around which the team could build its rotation. Through seven starts at the beginning of the 1988 season, Dravecky posted a 2–2 mark with a 3.16 ERA before doctors discovered a cancerous desmoids tumor in his left arm. Surgery was performed in October 1988, leaving Dravecky and the Giants optimistic about his chances of making a full recovery, while Dravecky's story captured a concerned nation. That recovery seemed to be going well once Dravecky began pitching again. In July 1989 his comeback advanced to where he was pitching in minor league games, which led to his return with the Giants on August 10 of that same year.

Dravecky made what appeared to be the beginning of a triumphant return when he picked up the win after pitching eight innings against the Reds in a 4–3 Giants win. But disaster struck in his next start five days later against the Montreal Expos. Prior to taking the mound in the sixth inning, Dravecky felt some tingling in his left arm. Damaso Garcia led off the inning with a home run before Dravecky hit the second batter, Andres Galarraga. After Dravecky released his first pitch to the next hitter, Tim Raines, he collapsed on the mound after the humerus bone in his left arm broke.

Dravecky did not surrender to the injury and began working toward a comeback while the bone healed. The final setback came after the Giants clinched the 1989 National League pennant when he again broke his arm during the celebration that took place on the mound. Further bad news came when doctors looked at X-rays of Dravecky's arm and discovered a mass; the cancer was back.

Baseball took a back seat to Dravecky's health, and he retired from the game with a career 64–57 record and a 3.13 ERA. A couple of surgeries followed, which eventually led to Dravecky having his left shoulder and arm amputated. Though devastated, the deeply religious Dravecky leaned on his faith and turned his tragedy into a positive. He has since served as an inspiration to many others while sharing his story as a motivational speaker.

31 Have a Beer at Lefty O'Doul's

Obviously, many dining and drinking option exist in San Francisco, but any true Giants fan needs to take a moment to have a cool one at Lefty O'Doul's, located downtown. Francis Joseph O'Doul, aka "Lefty," hailed from San Francisco and entered the major leagues as a pitcher in 1919 at the age of 22. Whether O'Doul would have had an extensive career as a pitcher will never be known since he injured his left arm during the 1923 season. What is known is that he became a pretty good hitter. After being out of the major leagues for five years, he returned as an outfielder with the Giants in 1928.

During his 11 seasons in the major leagues, O'Doul played for the Giants, New York Yankees, Boston Red Sox, Brooklyn Dodgers, and

Philadelphia Phillies, finishing with a lifetime .349 batting average. In 1929, when offense was skyrocketing all over baseball, O'Doul posted a career-high average of .398 while playing for the Phillies.

O'Doul's playing career ended in 1934 at the age of 37 when he hit .316 for the Giants. He managed the San Francisco Seals beginning in 1935. During his tenure at the helm of the Pacific Coast League team, he was a popular figure and helped direct a San Francisco kid named Joe DiMaggio to the major leagues. After managing the Seals for 17 seasons, Lefty O'Doul opened his establishment in 1958. Though Lefty died in 1969, O'Doul's remains a San Francisco treasure.

Unique baseball memorabilia and countless rare photos adorn the interior of Lefty O'Doul's, which will prompt most any baseball fan to want to grab his or her beer and take a stroll around the premises to carefully examine every one. There's plenty of cold beer, though the menu is not along the lines of most of today's restaurants. Hearty comfort food is the order of the day at Lefty O'Doul's. You can start with an order of eggs with bacon, ham, or sausage with home-style potatoes and toast ($8.25), and you don't have to wait until 9:00 or 10:00 AM to eat if you're an early riser, as they open at 7:00 AM. The rest of the day you can chow down on their regular specials, which include: turkey leg and stuffing ($6.49), turkey wing and stuffing ($5.49), spaghetti and meatballs ($6.49), spaghetti and meat sauce ($5.49), corned beef and cabbage ($8.49), and Polish sausage ($6.49).

TVs allow patrons to watch all the games, and if you're taking the kids to the game with you, don't worry about bringing them inside—the place has a family atmosphere. But don't expect a fern bar, because Lefty O'Doul's is not that. The feeling is more like the warm feeling of a broken-in catcher's mitt. Baseball is talked in Lefty O'Doul's, which will get any Giants fan in the perfect mood before heading to AT&T Park to watch the game. It's also a great place to talk about baseball after the game.

Lefty O'Doul's is open Monday through Saturday from 7:00 AM to midnight, and is located near Union Square at 333 Geary Street, a short cab ride or a robust walk from AT&T Park.

32 Read *Pitching in a Pinch*

Christy Mathewson remains one of the all-time pitching greats, and he played for the Giants, so acquiring a copy of *Pitching in a Pinch, or, Baseball from the Inside* by Christy Mathewson is a no-brainer for any Giants fan. First published in 1912 and later rereleased, *Pitching in a Pinch* is Christy Mathewson's ghostwritten insider account of baseball during the early part of the 1900s. Of course, the story of the book, its inception, journey, and rediscovery make for a nice part of the story.

During the winters of 1911 and 1912, Mathewson—though well educated—worked with John Wheeler, a newspaper syndicate operator, to pen a collection of articles about baseball from an insider. In 1912 all of the articles were gathered into a book titled *Pitching in a Pinch*. At some point after its publication, the book disappeared, like many books do. According to *Sports Illustrated*, New York baseball writers Neil Offen and Vic Ziegel discovered a catalog card for the book in the New York Public Library, making them feel like archeologists discovering a rare artifact on a dig, only they were baseball archeologists. Through the efforts of Offen and Ziegel, the book was republished. And though it took them three years for the project to move to completion, the wait was worthwhile, as delving inside the covers of this classic is akin to time traveling to another era of baseball.

You don't have to be a Giants fan to enjoy this one since it gives readers an idea about what baseball was like in the salad days of the major leagues, from how the game was played to insights on the players who played the game. Inside are anecdotes, biographical information, instructions, and social history about the era, as well as close-up looks at baseball ghosts from the past such as Honus Wagner, Rube Marquard, John McGraw, and Connie Mack. We're talking about an era of baseball before Babe Ruth turned the game upside down by supplanting "small ball" with the long ball.

Modern pitchers would be wise to digest Mathewson's take on pitching in a pinch. He writes that the pinch is basically the truest test of what a pitcher is made of, the "pinch" being when runners are on base and the heat is on. He notes that there are pitchers who are fine when the heat isn't on, but who cave once in the pinch. And, of course, there's Mathewson, who is the winningest right-hander in National League history with 373 career wins. If anything, reading this book will allow the reader to appreciate Mathewson's greatness. This guy lived as a movie-star handsome American hero and was greatly admired for his baseball skills, his intellect, and the fact he conducted himself as the consummate gentleman.

The language is more formal than anything written today, but that makes the book more a reflection of the time it represents. And though the book was ghostwritten, there is no question Mathewson's prints are on the work, as famed sportswriter Red Smith observed in his introduction: "Unlike some spooks of later vintage, Wheeler was conscientious enough to consult Matty before putting the pitcher's comments on paper."

33 Watch *The Fan*

Wesley Snipes in a Giants uniform stalked by Robert De Niro— you had me at hello. Whether you consider *The Fan* a good movie or not isn't the point, the point is, it's must-see cinema if you're a Giants fan.

Gil Renard, played by De Niro, works as a knife salesman, but he's a loose cannon, and his job is not going well. Couple that situation with the fact his family dynamic isn't so good, as his son lives with his mother, and all Renard has left is his obsession with baseball. Of course, any movie in which De Niro plays a gangster or an obsessed character is usually worth the price of admission, and he doesn't disappoint in this one. And where that obsession is concerned, Bobby Rayburn is front and center for Renard.

Rayburn is played by Snipes, who had played a baseball player before in *Major League*, the 1989 movie in which he starred as the base-stealing threat Willie Mays Hayes. Snipes resembled an athlete in that movie—though *Major League* was tainted with silliness that took away from certain parts—and he looks like an athlete wearing the uniform of the San Francisco Giants. Rayburn has a $40 million contract with the Giants and is everything Renard wants a baseball star to be. We see that Renard has followed Rayburn since Rayburn played high school baseball and has the newspaper clippings to prove it. Rayburn drives a Humvee, so Renard buys a model Humvee. No doubt this is love at first sight for Renard, who communicates with Rayburn from time to time through Jewel Stern's talk radio show; Stern is played credibly by Ellen Barkin.

Problems begin to arise when Rayburn goes into a tailspin. Eventually, this leads Renard to discover that Rayburn is simply a ballplayer and not some kind of god. This is not a good thing for Rayburn, because Renard would rather Rayburn be a god. Renard ends up kidnapping Rayburn's son, and Rayburn's pursuit to rescue his son from this stalker takes the film to its climax, which is disappointing given the authenticity throughout the film.

De Niro does a nice job of playing the stalker, who is so into his obsession that it becomes his life, which of course is what he's supposed to do since he's the title character. There are some wrong stadiums and uniforms in the film, but that's usually the case with any sports movie. What the film did get right for the most part was what happens inside the clubhouse, and there is a fairly accurate account of the relationship between a player and his agent. What makes the movie particularly disturbing was the fact that by the end of the movie you believe that a fan could actually become as deranged as De Niro's character.

The movie is rated R, and most parents would be best served to take a good look at this one before letting their kids watch it—even if they are Giants fans. De Niro's character is simply too believable and, in addition to his violent behavior, there are disturbing scenes within his own family situation.

 **Giants No-Hitters**

Jonathan Sanchez drew the starting assignment against the San Diego Padres on July 10, 2009, for one reason: Randy Johnson, who was supposed to start, had a sore left shoulder. Thus the Padres drew Sanchez rather than the "Big Unit." On the bright side for Sanchez and the Giants, the Padres' lineup was one of the more benign in the major leagues.

Everything has to fall right into place for any pitcher to throw a no-hitter. He must perform well and he must be lucky. Well, Sanchez ended up pitching a no-hitter in an 8–0 win, and where luck was concerned, he had none in the eighth. While flirting with a perfect game, third baseman Jose Uribe's error with one out in the eighth inning cost Sanchez the perfect game. However, the Giants left-hander received a healthy dose of luck in the ninth inning when Gold Glove center fielder Aaron Rowand saved the no-hitter by leaping to grab pinch-hitter Edgar Gonzalez's drive at the cent. field fence for the second out.

Once Sanchez's work was done, he became the 13th Giants pitcher to throw a no-hitter and the first since "the Count." The Count was John Montefusco, who received his nickname due to the closeness of his last name to "Monte Cristo," as in *The Count of Monte Cristo*. Montefusco's no-hitter came against the Atlanta Braves on September 29, 1976.

Amos Rusie became the first member of the Giants to throw a no-hitter when he turned the trick on July 31, 1891, against the Brooklyn Bridegrooms. Rusie would be inducted into the Baseball Hall of Fame by the Veterans Committee in 1977. Despite that fact, and the fact he won 234 games for the Giants, Giants fans know him better as the player who was traded to the Cincinnati Reds for Christy Mathewson prior to the 1901 season. Mathewson, of course, went on to 373 wins with the Giants, while Rusie suffered a career-ending injury early in the next season with the Reds.

While we're on the subject, Mathewson holds the record for the most no-hitters by a Giants pitcher with two. Mathewson's first no-hitter came at St. Louis against the Cardinals on July 15, 1901, during a 5–0 Giants win. The Giants' all-time winningest pitcher then threw another no-hitter on June 13, 1905, against the Cubs in Chicago during a 1–0 Giants win.

George "Hooks" Wiltse became the first left-handed Giants pitcher to throw a no-hitter when he held the Philadelphia Phillies hitless on July 4, 1908, in a 1–0 win that took 10 innings to complete. Jeff Tesreau, Rube Marquard, and Jesse Barnes followed with the fifth, sixth, and seventh no-hitters in team history before "King Carl" came through with a no-hitter on May 8, 1929. Carl Hubbell, a Hall of Fame inductee in 1947, held the Pittsburgh Pirates hitless at the Polo Grounds during an 11–0 win. Hubbell's no-hitter would be the last pitched while the Giants played in New York.

against the Giants

tched the Giants' last no-hitter when he pulled off the feat
ganization 13 no-hitters in their storied history. However,
and black has found itself on the other side of the coin, too, as
opposing pitchers have tossed 15 no-hitters against the Giants. Here are the
no-hitters that have been pitched against the Giants:

Date	Opponent	Pitcher	Score
June 22, 1891	at Brooklyn Bridegrooms	Tom Lovett	4–0
May 25, 1899	at Louisville Colonels	Deacon Phillippe	7–0
Aug. 31, 1915	vs. Chicago Cubs (1st game)	Jimmy Lavender	2–0
Sept. 9, 1948	vs. Brooklyn Dodgers	Rex Barney	2–0
May 12, 1956	at Brooklyn Dodgers	Carl Erskine	3–0
April 28, 1961	at Milwaukee Braves	Warren Spahn	1–0
May 11, 1963	at Los Angeles Dodgers	Sandy Koufax	8–0
Sept. 18, 1968	vs. St. Louis Cardinals	Ray Washburn	2–0
June 27, 1980	vs. Los Angeles Dodgers	Jerry Reuss	8–0
May 10, 1981	at Montreal Expos (2nd game)	Charlie Lea	4–0
Sept. 25, 1986	at Houston Astros	Mike Scott	2–0
Aug. 15, 1990	at Philadelphia Phillies	Terry Mulholland	6–0
Aug. 17, 1992	at Los Angeles Dodgers	Kevin Gross	2–0
June 10, 1997	vs. Florida Marlins	Kevin Brown	9–0
April 27, 2003	at Philadelphia Phillies	Kevin Millwood	1–0

Another Hall of Famer followed Hubbell as the next Giants pitcher to throw a no-hitter when Juan Marichal no-hit the Houston Colt .45s in a 1–0 Giants win at Candlestick Park on June 15, 1963. The "Dominican Dandy" had five strikeouts in the game, and none was sweeter than his fifth. Brock Davis went down looking to end the game, and Marichal had the first no-hitter for the Giants since moving to San Francisco.

The trail of Giants no-hitters pitched by Hall of Fame pitchers continued when Gaylord Perry no-hit the Cardinals for a 1–0 win at Candlestick Park on September 17, 1968. Making that accomplishment even more noteworthy was the fact that Hall of Famer Bob Gibson pitched a complete-game four-hitter against the Giants that same day. In addition, the last out came via a strikeout when Curt Flood watched a third strike. Of note, Ron Hunt's home run in the first inning was the only run of the game; Hunt hit just two home runs that season. In a strange turn of events, the Giants were the victims of a no-hitter the following day when Ray Washburn turned the trick, 2–0.

Prior to Montefusco's no-hitter, Ed Halicki no-hit the New York Mets on August 24, 1975, as the Giants won 6–0 in the second game of a doubleheader.

Giants Retired Numbers

The Giants' history dates back to 1882, but despite the many years the team has operated in the major leagues, only 11 former players and managers have had their jersey numbers retired by the team. No other team in baseball, save for the New York Yankees who have retired 15, has more retired numbers. The following are the players and managers who have been recognized over the years by the Giants organization by having their uniform numbers retired:

Christy Mathewson—played for the Giants from 1900 to 1916 and remains the organization's all-time leader in wins, complete games, shutouts, innings, and strikeouts. He went into the Baseball Hall of Fame posthumously in 1936 as part of Cooperstown's inaugural class. While his number is retired in theory, an actual number is not retired for him since players did not wear numbers when Mathewson played.

John McGraw—served with the Giants as player/manager from 1902 to 1906 and remained the team's skipper until 1932. He is the franchise's all-time winningest manager. Like Mathewson, he did not have a number to be retired.

Bill Terry—wore No. 3 and played for the Giants from 1923 to 1936. His .401 batting average in 1930 is the highest in franchise history and also marked the last time a National League player hit over .400. He was enshrined in the Hall of Fame in 1954.

Mel Ott—wore No. 4 and played for the Giants from 1926 to 1947. He is the franchise's all-time RBI leader and ranks second in games played. He was inducted into the Hall of Fame in 1951.

Carl Hubbell—wore No. 11 and played for the Giants from 1928 to 1943. Hubbell was a nine-time All-Star, and his 1933 ERA of 1.66 is the 10th best in franchise history. He was inducted into the Hall of Fame in 1947.

Willie Mays—wore No. 24 and played for the Giants from 1951 to 1972. Appeared in 24 All-Star Games and was a two-time National League MVP. He is the franchise's all-time leader in home runs and games played. He was inducted into the Hall of Fame in 1979.

Juan Marichal—wore No. 27 and played for the Giants from 1960 to 1973. A nine-time All-Star, his 238 wins are the most by any pitcher after the team moved to San Francisco. He was inducted into the Hall of Fame in 1983.

Orlando Cepeda—wore No. 30 and played for the Giants from 1958 to 1966. Was a six-time All-Star as a Giant and earned Rookie of the Year honors in 1958. He still holds the single-season RBI mark for the Giants in San Francisco with 142 in 1961. He was inducted into the Hall of Fame in 1999.

Pick Your Own All-Time Team

Few sports fans agree with sportswriters when it comes to the selection of All-Star teams, all-decade teams or all-time teams. So why not skip the sportswriters and come up with your own all-time Giants team?

Wait until you can gather a decent-sized crowd of your buddies who also share your passion for the team, then conduct a vote just like the baseball writers do for postseason awards. In the case of the Giants, it would be fun to vote on three such teams: the all-time New York Giants, the all-time San Francisco Giants, and the all-time Giants. Vote for the best player at each position, including three outfielders, left- and right-handed starting pitchers, and a closer.

Each participant gets a pad of paper and votes on the top three at each position for all three teams. A first-place vote yields five points; second place, three points; and third place, one point. The player with the highest amount of points is the winner. Prior to passing out the pads and pencils is when the open forum takes place in which a healthy exchange of ideas can circulate. For example, most would recognize Christy Mathewson as the greatest right-hander for the Giants, but would Juan Marichal or Tim Lincecum take that spot on the all-time San Francisco team?

Some other interesting debates could come at first base. Bill Terry would likely be anybody's pick for the New York Giants, and Willie McCovey for the San Francisco Giants. But which one do you pick as your all-time Giants selection? Terry once hit .401, while McCovey hit 521 career home runs, 469 of which came with the Giants.

Finally, will your group vote Willie Mays to all three teams?

All of these questions lead to healthy debate, a lot of beer and snacks being consumed, and at the end of the day you will have elected your own all-time Giants teams—sportswriters be damned.

Gaylord Perry—wore No. 36 and played for the Giants from 1962 to 1971. He ranks second in the team's history in San Francisco in wins, ERA, games started, complete games, shutouts, innings pitched, and strikeouts. He was inducted into the Hall of Fame in 1991.

Willie McCovey—wore No. 44 and played for the Giants from 1959 to 1973 and from 1977 to 1980. A six-time All-Star, he earned Rookie of the Year honors in 1959 and Most Valuable Player honors in 1969. He was inducted into the Hall of Fame in 1986.

Monte Irvin—wore No. 20 and, along with Hank Thompson, was one of the first African Americans to play for the Giants, as both joined the team in 1949. In 1951 Irvin helped lead the Giants to a National League pennant when he had 121 RBIs.

The Giants also honored Jackie Robinson, whose uniform No. 42 was retired by every team in Major League Baseball in 1997 to commemorate the 50th anniversary of his arrival to the major leagues.

36 Experience McCovey Cove

If you're looking for something a little different, McCovey Cove is the place to be during Giants home games. But you better not mind a little bit of water, because chances are you're going to get wet. McCovey Cove is a part of AT&T Park, but not really. It's the name of the area beyond the right-field wall, which actually is part of San Francisco Bay.

Yes, the area is named, though not officially, for former Giants slugger Willie McCovey, who once hit his home runs at Candlestick Park far over the right-field wall. China Basin is the actual name for the cove, but due to the ideas and efforts of sportswriters Mark Purdy and Leonard Koppett, the area has come to be known as McCovey Cove. Purdy, who worked for the *San Jose Mercury News*, suggested in print that the area on the water outside right field be named for McCovey. He had that part right, but his suggestions coupled with McCovey's name simply did not work. Koppett, of the *Oakland Tribune*, suggested "McCovey Cove," and the name stuck.

McCovey Cove, beyond the right-field bleachers at AT&T Park (formerly PacBell Park), where many a Giants home run has splashed down.

The idea is to take in a Giants game while in the waters of McCovey Cove by sitting in a raft, a row boat, or some sort of flotation device. If you are there on a good day, you might collect a home run ball that clears the right-field portion of the stadium and plunks into the water. Balls that are hit into the water become "splash hits," which can only be officially recorded by Giants players.

But hitting a ball over the right-field wall and into McCovey Cove is no easy task. Take the 2007 Home Run Derby held at AT&T Park during the 2007 All-Star Game. Everybody figured the waters of McCovey Cove would be peppered throughout the contest. But at the end of the day, only Milwaukee Brewers slugger Prince Fielder had managed to launch one into the water, and that one was foul.

The all-time leader of splash hits is Barry Bonds, who had 35, many of which were prominent home runs during his chase for the single-season home run record, which he set in 2001, and when he went for the career home run mark in 2007. Bonds' number is remarkable, considering the total number of splash hits had not reached 60 by the end of the 2010 season. Aside from Bonds, the only other Giants players to have accomplished a splash hit more than once are Michael Tucker, Felipe Crespo, Ryan Klesko, Pablo Sandoval, Aubrey Huff, and Andres Torres. Sandoval actually hit the 49th and 50th splash hits a month apart in 2009.

Carlos Delgado leads the contingent of opposing players to hit a baseball into the cove, as he accomplished the feat three times. Luis Gonzalez and Cliff Floyd each reached the water twice for opposing teams.

While on the surface the idea of seeing how many baseballs you can land seems to be the object of spending an afternoon outside the ballpark in the waters of McCovey Cove, that simply isn't the case. And if you go there believing that, you'll be, uh, missing the boat. The idea is to get out in the water with the sun baking your face, while mingling with other fans who happen to share the idea that the Giants are the best thing going. Should a baseball find its way to your part of the water, that should be viewed as a bonus for a great day at the ballpark—or outside of it.

37 Gaylord Perry

Gaylord Perry became notorious for his use of the spitball, but during his days wearing a San Francisco Giants uniform he was known for having quality stuff and for being one of the best pitchers in club history.

In 1958 the Giants signed Perry to a contract that included an unusually large bonus for the time—$90,000. He first reached the major leagues in 1962 at the age of 23 but hardly got off to an auspicious beginning. He made 13 appearances that first season—seven were starts—and he posted a 3–1 record with a 5.23 ERA. The next season he appeared in 31 games, making just four starts, and went 1–6 with a 4.03 ERA. Despite the less-than-stellar numbers, Perry's talents were evident to the Giants, so they afforded him the opportunity to join the starting rotation in 1964. He responded by going 12–11 with a 2.75 ERA. Perry likely would have gained more acclaim in the rotation had he not played second fiddle to Juan Marichal.

He regressed in 1965 when he finished at 8–12, but again, the Giants liked his stuff, so they stuck with him. He rewarded their faith with a big season in 1966, when he went 21–8 with a 2.99 ERA. Unfortunately for Perry, even though those were tremendous numbers, he did not finish strong. The right-hander had a 20–2 record in late August, but managed to win just one more game, finishing the final two months with a 1–6 mark.

Marichal struggled with injuries in 1967, which propelled Perry to the role of No. 1 starter, and he had a difficult time handling the top spot. His record slumped to 15–17 that season, though he posted a sterling 2.61 ERA. He improved in 1968 to go 16–15 with a 2.45 ERA. That same season he tossed a no-hitter against the Cardinals on September 17. He then had seasons of 19–14 and 23–13 in 1969 and 1970, finally establishing himself as one of the best pitchers in baseball.

In Perry's final season with the Giants in 1971, he posted a 16–12 record with a 2.76 ERA, which helped the Giants win the National League West division. Perry would make the only postseason appearances of his career that season, winning one against the Pittsburgh Pirates and losing the other as the Pirates advanced to the World Series.

Scoreless Streak

Giants fans sat in awe as Tim Lincecum posted a career-best scoreless streak from June 23, 2009, to July 9, 2009. The Giants right-hander went 29 consecutive innings without allowing a run. And Giants fans should have been in awe: going that many innings without allowing a run is truly a pitching feat. Lincecum's streak was the longest in the major leagues in 2009 and was one inning longer than teammate Jeremy Affeldt's 28-inning streak.

Lincecum's streak, however, was not the longest in San Francisco Giants history. Juan Marichal had a 30-inning streak in 1966, and Gaylord Perry had a 39-inning streak in 1970. But the longest streak in San Francisco Giants history came when Perry went 40 innings without allowing a run in 1967. He began his streak on August 28 with a three-hit shutout of the Los Angeles Dodgers. Four days later, he pitched 16 scoreless innings but did not get a decision in a game the Giants eventually won 1–0 over the Cincinnati Reds in 21 innings. On September 6, Perry continued to dominate with a three-hitter against the Astros at Candlestick Park that extended his streak to 34 consecutive scoreless innings. On September 10, during a Sunday afternoon game at Candlestick Park, Perry faced Chicago and posted six scoreless innings before the Cubs scored an unearned run in the seventh when Ron Santo scored during a double-play. Perry went on to pitch a complete game three-hitter. Amazingly, Perry had pitched eight shutout innings on August 24, four days in advance of the beginning of his streak. But he allowed two runs in the ninth inning to take a 2–0 loss to the Cardinals that game.

Carl Hubbell owns the Giants franchise record with 46⅓ scoreless innings, which he set in 1933 as a New York Giant. Orel Hershiser, of the archrival Los Angeles Dodgers, set the major league record for consecutive scoreless innings pitched when he tossed 59⅓ straight scoreless innings in 1988.

Prior to the 1972 season, Perry was traded to the Cleveland Indians. In 10 seasons with the Giants, he went 134–109 with a 2.96 ERA. In addition to playing for the Indians, he would go on to play for the Texas Rangers, San Diego Padres, Atlanta Braves, Seattle Mariners, New York Yankees, and Kansas City Royals, finishing his 22-year career with a record of 314–265 and a 3.11 ERA.

While Perry admitted to throwing the spitball, he would play mind games with the hitters the older he got, going through all kinds of motions as if he were loading up the baseball with a wet one. The ritual worked on the hitters, who wondered if they were seeing a spitball or not. Perry was a five-time All-Star and became the first pitcher to win the Cy Young Award in both leagues, winning the award in the American League while pitching for the Indians in 1972 and in 1978 while pitching for the Padres. Perry and his brother, Jim, rank behind the Niekro brothers, Phil and Joe, in the most wins in the major leagues by brothers. In 1991 Gaylord Perry was elected to the Baseball Hall of Fame.

Monte Irvin

Jackie Robinson had already broke baseball's color barrier by the time Monte Irvin joined the New York Giants in 1949, but make no mistake about it, the native of Alabama was a pioneer in his own right as he was one of the first black players to be signed after Robinson's entry. Irvin began his career in the Negro Leagues in 1938 with the Newark Eagles, where he distinguished himself in a league full of stars. Irvin hit an incredible .422 for the Eagles in 1940 and followed that season's excellence by hitting .396 in 1941.

Being a professional baseball player, Irvin went where the money was best in 1943, which meant Mexico, and all he did was hit .397 to lead the league in hitting while earning the Most Valuable Player award. Though he played baseball in a country that saw no problem with segregation in the major leagues, Irvin fulfilled his patriotic duty by serving in the military for two years during World War II before returning to the Eagles to resume his excellence by hitting .401 in 1946 to win the league batting championship for the second time.

Shortly after Irvin's military service was complete, Brooklyn Dodgers executive Branch Rickey approached him about signing to play for the Dodgers. Irvin might have signed the deal had he not felt he was rusty after being away from the game for two seasons. Instead, he opted to spend time playing in Puerto Rico and Cuba. Approximately two years after Rickey made overtures to Irvin, the Giants bought Irvin's contract. He played briefly in 1949 before returning to the Giants in 1950. At the age of 31, Irvin hit .299 with 15 home runs and 66 RBIs in his first full season with the Giants.

Irvin played outfield and first base in 1951, while helping lead the Giants to the National League pennant by hitting .312 with 24 home runs and a league-leading 121 RBIs. The Giants lost to the Yankees in the World Series, but nobody could blame Irvin, who hit .458 against the Yankees, getting 11 hits in 24 at-bats. After the season, Irvin finished third in the National League's Most Valuable Player voting that season.

Of note, the Giants set a precedent in 1951 with Irvin playing his part when he started in the outfield alongside Willie Mays and Hank Thompson, thereby creating the major league's first all–African American outfield. Irvin hit for his highest average as a Giant in 1953 when he hit .329. And in 1954, at the age of 35, Irvin again helped lead the Giants to a National League pennant. This time, when the Giants reached the World Series, they came away winners after sweeping the Cleveland Indians.

Irvin played his final season with the Giants in 1955 before spending the final year of his career with the Cubs in 1956. In eight major league seasons, Irvin hit .293 with 99 home runs and 443 RBIs. Irvin was inducted into the Baseball Hall of Fame in 1973, which was due largely to his career in the Negro Leagues. Irvin remained in baseball after his playing days, serving in various positions for teams as well as in the commissioner's office. The Giants held a ceremony at AT&T Park to honor Irvin before the game that took place on June 26, 2010. With Hall of Fame former Giants Juan Marichal, Gaylord Perry, Willie Mays, Willie McCovey, and Orlando Cepeda in attendance, Irvin had his No. 20 uniform retired.

39 Attend a Game at AT&T Park

The home of the Giants had several names before being tagged "AT&T Park" in 2006. By any name, this open-air baseball cathedral is a major upgrade over the Giants' former home—the meat locker known as Candlestick Park. The Giants' former park had a well-earned reputation for making anyone feel like the coldest winter they'd ever experienced was a summer at Candlestick Park. While AT&T can get cold, it is not a slave to the wind like Candlestick had been, which has resulted in an overall climate for watching baseball a bit milder than something out of a Jack London novel.

Location is also a major upgrade, as the park is located at 24 Willie Mays Plaza, at the corner of Third and King Streets, in the South Beach neighborhood of San Francisco. AT&T Park cost $357 million, which included the work of engineers to come up with a design where the wind would not be as much of a factor as it had been at Candlestick. The resulting design devised a structure that significantly reduced wind levels from those at the Giants' former home.

No public funds were used in building the park, which opened on March 31, 2000. Fittingly, the first game played at PacBell Park—AT&T's original name—was against the Los Angeles Dodgers on April 11, 2000. Kevin Elster hit three home runs for the Dodgers as L.A. won 6–5. Though a relatively young ballpark, AT&T has hosted a number of memorable events and accomplishments, such as those of Barry Bonds. The Giants slugger hit his 500th and 600th home runs there, in addition to setting the single-season home run mark of 73, hitting his 715th home run to surpass

Good-Bye, San Francisco

Nobody in San Francisco would dispute the fact that the Giants needed a new stadium in the late 1980s. Candlestick Park had grown old, and the facility had never been the best to host a baseball game, given the brutal swirling winds that accompanied most games. However, recognizing the need for a new facility and paying for a new facility were two different things.

Shortly after the Giants lost to the Oakland A's in the 1989 World Series, a local ballot initiative to fund a new San Francisco stadium did not pass, which left the team's ownership with a couple of options. They could continue to operate the team at Candlestick Park and hope that attendance would somehow improve. They could move the team to an area that would support the team. They could build a new stadium themselves. Or they could sell the team. In 1992 the Giants ownership chose to sell the team to a group of investors from St. Petersburg, Florida. Led by Vince Naimoli, the St. Petersburg group reached an agreement to purchase the team and relocate them to an already built indoor facility in St. Petersburg. However, National League owners voted against the acquisition and made sure that a deal got made in which the team got sold to a San Francisco ownership group headed by Peter Magowan.

With the sale came the promise of moving the team to a new facility in San Francisco's downtown area. In addition, the new Giants ownership made a bold move to improve their existing team by signing Barry Bonds to a megadeal prior to the 1993 season. Suddenly, the Giants had managed to find stability. Now that the team has moved to AT&T Park, it's hard to imagine the Giants ever struggling again or considering a move to another area.

Babe Ruth's career mark, and his 756th to surpass Hank Aaron's career mark to become the all-time home run king.

The 2007 All-Star Game was held in the park, as were Games 3, 4, and 5 of the 2002 World Series when the Giants played the Anaheim Angels, and Games 1 and 2 of the 2010 Series against the Rangers, which the Giants ultimately clinched at Texas in Game 5.

Jonathan Sanchez's no-hitter on July 10, 2009, became the first pitched at the park. In addition to being the home of the Giants, AT&T Park hosts other events, such as concerts. The Rolling Stones, Kenny Chesney, Metallica, Dave Mathews Band, Bruce Springsteen, and Paul McCartney have all performed at the venue.

AT&T Park has a seating capacity of 41,606, which includes 68 luxury suits, 5,200 club seats on the club level, and 1,500 club seats behind home plate at field level.

In honor of Giants great No. 24, Willie Mays, the right-field wall stands 24 feet tall, providing the most distinctive portion of the ballpark. Balls hit by Giants players that clear the wall and land in the area of water outside the ballpark known as McCovey Cove are honored as "splash hits" (see No. 36, "Experience McCovey Cove").

Giants greats are honored along the facing of the upper deck down the left-field line as the retired numbers of McCovey, Gaylord Perry, Orlando Cepeda, Juan Marichal, Mays, Carl Hubbell, Bill Terry, and Mel Ott are all featured there, as well as Jackie Robinson's No. 42. To honor John McGraw and Christy Mathewson, who were in the game before jersey numbers, an "NY" takes their place.

To enhance the fan experience, the Giants installed 122 wireless Internet points, which makes AT&T Park a huge public hotspot. In addition, the food is exceptional (see No. 66, "Pig Out at AT&T Park"). In short, there is very little to be disappointed with while attending a game at AT&T Park, other than the score of the game if the Giants lose.

40 Attend a Spring Training Game in Scottsdale

Spring training is a perfect time of year for any Giants fan. After spending the winter reading and watching reports about the improvements the team has made during the off-season, you can head for Scottsdale and see how the Giants' nine look once they are finally assembled.

Scottsdale Stadium in Scottsdale, Arizona, is the place the Giants call home for their Cactus League season, which begins annually in the first part of March. Like most spring training stadiums, Scottsdale Stadium offers fans a better chance to feel close to the players. Normally, players will sign autographs before and after games, and they always seemed to be a little more hospitable before the regular season begins. Meanwhile, the actual outcome of the game should not be the most important part of the day for the fan, because it certainly is not for the player.

For Giants fans, a spring training game at Scottsdale Stadium has a lot to offer. For starters, there is the relaxed atmosphere. Attending a game is a great way to get the knots out. Most games are played under sunny skies in mild temperatures with beer and hot dogs a mere trip to the concession stand away. If you want to see the Giants' regulars, you don't want to be a late arrival to the game since the games played during the early part of spring training usually feature the starters for five or fewer innings. During those innings, you don't want to be too judgmental, since the idea is to get into shape for the regular season. Which means if Tim Lincecum is getting lit up, chances are he's just throwing fastballs or he's going through the dreaded "dead arm" period all pitchers go through during spring training—it's not a bellwether for the coming season.

Meanwhile, don't get too happy if that rookie sensation is hitting a lot of home runs. While they are swinging at major league fastballs, knowing that a fastball is coming is a great deal easier than when the pitchers are mixing up their offerings. In other words, if a rookie hits 10 homers in 20 spring training games, don't count on him to break Barry Bonds' home run record during the regular season.

Late innings at spring training games belong to the up-and-comers of the organization. Often the seventh, eighth, and ninth innings are the best part of the game because the youngsters are playing to make an impression. Take the time to learn who these youngsters are, and you'll be greatly rewarded. Most of the youngsters already know they are earmarked for the minor leagues at the beginning of the season, but they also know that making an impression on the major league manager with their hustle or skills could help earn a promotion later in the season.

Scottsdale Stadium is a terrific venue for watching the games. Built in 1992, the park was renovated in 2006 to the tune of $23.1 million, which put in place an agreement for the Giants to remain in Scottsdale through 2025 with an option to extend the lease for 10 additional years. Some interesting features of the park include terrace seating in the right-field berm area and a walkway that connects the right- and left-field berms.

Nearby practice facilities also allow fans to view different aspects of spring training, like when one of the team's pitchers makes a start against a minor league club so he can get his work in, or during the time before the actual beginning of spring training games when the team goes through daily workouts.

41 Leo Durocher

Leo Durocher was not a well-loved man. He cared about winning games, not friends, which is what worked for him while becoming one of the winningest managers in major league history. Leo the Lip's famous creed was: "Nice guys finish last."

Like many successful managers, Durocher had limited talents as a player—particularly as a hitter. He used what talent he had and managed to cobble together a lengthy major league career. Personifying his lack of hitting talent was the nickname Babe Ruth hung on him after Durocher was called to the major leagues by the New York Yankees in 1925. The Bambino referred to Durocher as "the All-American Out."

Leo "the Lip" Durocher, demonstrating the source of his nickname from the top step of the Giants dugout at the Polo Grounds in New York.

While Durocher might have had little talent as a hitter, he had the other talents, such as a combative attitude and a cocksure manner, and he was a gifted bench jockey. In addition, he had the necessary baseball intellect to be a manager. Yankees manager Miller Huggins first recognized those qualities in Durocher when he played for the Yankees until they sold him to the Cincinnati Reds prior to the 1930 season. Durocher had other, less admirable qualities, as well, such as a propensity for kiting checks to support a fancy wardrobe, a penchant for enjoying the nightlife, and all that being a part of the culture entailed. Having limited talents and being a problem off the field equated to a well-traveled career that saw him play for the Yankees, Reds, St. Louis Cardinals, and Brooklyn Dodgers. While with the Cardinals, he played for a group known as "the Gashouse Gang," which reflected his style of play. They would do anything to win, including going days without washing their uniforms during winning streaks. Durocher thrived in that setting, and the Cardinals were successful on the field.

Playing shortstop for the most part throughout his playing days, Durocher's career stretched through the 1945 season, and he finished with a .247 career batting average in 5,350 at-bats with 567 RBIs. During his career, he made the National League All-Star team three times.

Durocher's first stint as a manager came with the Dodgers in 1939 while still a player for the team. In his third season as manager, Durocher led the Dodgers to the National League pennant in 1941 before they lost to the Yankees in the World Series. He remained the Dodgers manager through 1946 before he received a one-year suspension from baseball, which he served during the 1947 season for being associated with known gamblers.

While Durocher was away from the Dodgers, Burt Shotton served as the team's interim manager and guided the team to the National League pennant before losing to the Yankees in the World Series. Durocher returned during the 1948 season and had little success with the Dodgers, which prompted an odd arrangement that saw the Dodgers and Giants agree to a deal that sent Durocher to the Giants as their new manager.

Durocher experienced his best years as a manager while with the Giants, leading the team to National League pennants in 1951 and 1954. In 1954 the Giants faced the heavily favored Cleveland Indians in the World Series and pulled off the upset, sweeping the American League team that had won a record 111 games that season.

Durocher left the Giants after the 1955 season, finishing his stint as the team's manager with a record of 637–523. He worked as a baseball broadcaster with NBC before returning as a coach with the Dodgers from 1961 through 1964. He went on to manage the Chicago Cubs and the Houston Astros and later had a short stint as a manager in Japan before he retired due to health reasons. Durocher's career record as a manager was 2,008–1,709, and he had the distinction of becoming the first major league manager to win more than 500 games with three different teams (Dodgers, Giants, and Cubs). On October 7, 1991, Durocher died in Palm Springs, California, at the age of 86. Three years later, in 1994, he was elected posthumously to the Baseball Hall of Fame by the Veterans Committee.

42 Merkle's Boner

Fred Merkle had never started a major league game when John McGraw gave him the starting nod on September 23, 1908. Regular first baseman Fred Tenney suffered from lumbago, prompting the Giants manager to use Merkle in his place for that day's game against the Chicago Cubs. Merkle was the youngest player in the National League at 19, and what a memorable start he would make that day.

The Giants and Cubs were tied for first place on the morning of September 23, and the Pittsburgh Pirates were not far behind with time running out in the season. Only two umpires were on the field that day, which was the norm for that period in the major leagues. What happened that day would bring compelling arguments in the future for having expanded umpiring crews.

In the bottom of the ninth, with the Giants batting and two out, Moose McCormick hugged first base, representing the winning run, when Merkle stepped into the batter's box. For Merkle, the at-bat represented his biggest as a major leaguer to that date, and he responded to the pressure situation with a single down the right-field line that allowed McCormick to reach third.

The crowd at the Polo Grounds could smell the victory with Al Bridwell hitting. And the Giants shortstop came through, stroking a single through the middle off Jack Pfiester. McCormick scored easily from third, and the Giants had a 2–1 victory, or so they thought.

Cubs shortstop Johnny Evers observed the action as Giants fans poured onto the field. And he noticed that in all the excitement, Merkle had failed to touch second base. Evers knew the rules, and under official rule 4.09, "a run is not scored if the runner advances to home base during a play in which the third out is made…by any runner being forced out." While this rule was not normally enforced on walk-off hits back in 1908, Evers saw a window of opportunity and yelled to the Cubs center fielder Solly Hofman to throw him the baseball. According to some reports, Giants pitcher Joe McGinnity, who coached first base for the team that day, saw what Evers was trying to do and stepped in front of Hofman's relay to Evers, catching the ball and then throwing it into the mob of fans. Even if McGinnity managed to do so, Evers somehow came up with the baseball—or perhaps another ball—and proceeded to second base, where he stepped on the bag.

Observing what had transpired on the field, the umpires ruled that Merkle had not touched second and called him out as a result. So the winning run did not score, and the game was ruled a 1–1 tie due to darkness. Many different accounts of what happened because of "Merkle's Boner" turned the game into a full-blown controversy with the outcome of the National League pennant race hanging in the breech.

The National League board of directors made their final ruling on the game that Merkle had not touched second base. Two weeks later, both teams finished with records of 98–55, which mandated that a makeup game be played to decide the tie game. The Cubs won the makeup game 4–2, crowning them as the National League champions for the third consecutive season. From there, the Cubs defeated the Detroit Tigers in the 1908 World Series.

Merkle went on to play 16 seasons in the major leagues. When his career ended after the 1926 season, he disappeared from the baseball scene due in large part to the one episode that stained his career. But in 1950 he appeared at a Giants old-timers' game and received a standing ovation.

43 Dusty Baker

For someone who always played for the enemy—save for a brief stint with the Giants in 1984, Dusty Baker proved to be one of the more popular managers the Giants have had since they moved to San Francisco. That's because Baker possessed a likeable personality, and his teams won baseball games.

Baker began his professional career as an outfielder with the Atlanta Braves at the age of 19 in 1968. He spent eight seasons with the Braves, hitting .278 with 77 home runs and 324 RBIs. Baker played alongside Hank Aaron in the Braves' outfield and was the hitter standing on deck when Aaron hit his history-making 715th home run, which broke Babe Ruth's career home run mark.

Baker moved to the Dodgers in 1976, where he would play in three World Series, including the Dodgers' world championship in 1981. He spent eight seasons with the Dodgers, hitting .281 with 144 home runs and 586 RBIs, then finished his career with stints playing for the Giants and Athletics. He retired following the 1986 season, finishing a solid major league career with a .278 average, 242 home runs, and 1,013 RBIs. In addition, he played for the National League All-Star team in 1981 and 1982. Of note, Baker hit his 30th home run of the season on the final day of the 1977 season, earning the Dodgers the distinction of being the first team in major league history to have four players with 30 or more home runs.

Baker paid his dues en route to becoming the Giants manager. First he served as the team's first-base coach in 1988, followed by four seasons as the team's hitting coach. In 1993 Baker became the manager of the Giants and earned National League Manager of the Year honors after he led the team to a second-place finish with a 103–59 record. Baker's Giants won National League West division titles in 1997 and 2000, when he won his second and third Manager of the Year awards.

In 2002 Baker got his Giants to claw their way into the playoffs as a wild-card team, and they plowed through the National League playoffs to earn a spot in the World Series, where they faced the Anaheim Angels, also a wild-card team (see No. 56, "Two Wild-Cards in the World Series"). In reaching the Series, Baker became one of two African Americans to be the manager of a World Series team; Cito Gaston, who managed the Toronto Blue Jays to two World Series championships in 1992 and 1993, is the other. Despite taking a 3–2 lead in the Series, the Giants lost in seven games.

That would be Baker's final season with the Giants, who allowed him to go to Chicago to become the manager of the Cubs in 2003, while the Giants hired Felipe Alou to take over the team. All told, Baker managed 1,556 games for the Giants in 10 seasons, compiling a record of 840–715. Baker went on to manage the Cubs for four seasons before moving on to manage the Reds in 2008.

44 Jack Clark

Jack Clark tiptoed into the major leagues with the Giants in 1975 at the age of 19, but it wouldn't be long before pitchers feared him, and he had acquired the nickname "Jack the Ripper." Clark had entered the Giants organization at the age of 17 after being drafted in the 13th round of the 1973 Major League Baseball June draft. He played right field and even pitched some for Great Falls in the Pioneer Rookie League, but the obvious strength of Clark's game was his bat.

Clark's early call to the show came after he hit .303 with 23 home runs and 77 RBIs for Double A Lafayette in 1975. After a cup of coffee with the Giants, he returned to Triple A the following season, hitting .323 with 17 home runs and 86 RBIs before once again getting the call to San Francisco.

Standing 6'2", 175 pounds, Clark hit 13 home runs with 51 RBIs in his first full season in the major leagues in 1977. The numbers Clark posted in the years that followed in no way reflected how hard he hit the ball or what a menacing force he was to deal with, which could be largely attributed to the cruel winds of Candlestick Park that turned back even some of Clark's most wicked drives. In 1978 at the age of 22, Clark hit .306 with 25 home runs and 98 RBIs in one of his best seasons for the Giants. He made the National League All-Star team that season and finished fifth in the National League Most Valuable Player voting.

Clark would spend 10 seasons with the Giants, from 1975 to 1984, playing right field and first base. Unfortunately for Clark, he played for the team during a dismal period in team history, which saw the Giants put together just three winning seasons in 10 years. For Clark, the losing was difficult. Remember, this is a man who, in his early years, said: "I have two goals. The first is to play in the World Series and the second is to hit .400. And I think I'll do both—someday." In addition to the losing, Candlestick Park beat him down as it did many hitters who saw would-be home runs in any other ballpark turn into routine fly-outs.

On February 1, 1985, the Giants shipped Clark to the St. Louis Cardinals for pitcher Dave LaPoint, first basemen/outfielders Gary Rajsich and David Green, and shortstop Jose Uribe. While playing

Jack Clark stands ready at the plate during a 1983 game. Jack "the Ripper" played for the Giants from 1975 to 1984 and made the All-Star team twice.

first base for the Cardinals, Clark had a role in one of the more notorious plays in World Series history. He made the toss to Cardinals reliever Todd Worrell covering first base in Game 6 of the 1985 World Series. Umpire Don Denkinger missed the call on the play, which enabled the Kansas City Royals to rally and win Game 6 before taking Game 7 to win the Series.

Clark's best season came with the Cardinals in 1987 when he hit .286 with 35 home runs and 106 RBIs to lead the Cardinals to the World Series. But an ankle injury prevented him from playing; he had just one at-bat during the postseason, and the Cardinals lost to the Minnesota Twins in the World Series. Clark finished his career with stints playing for the New York Yankees, San Diego Padres, and Boston Red Sox.

He remains one of the biggest what-if figures in the history of the Giants. What if the Giants had any kind of talent when they came up with a homegrown product the stature of Clark? Surely, the results would have been interesting.

Roger Craig

Roger Craig had a modest major league career, and like many before him who were hardly the glory of their time as players, the native of Durham, North Carolina, made an excellent major league manager. The Giants became the beneficiary of Craig's managerial prowess.

A right-handed pitcher with an above-average split-fingered fastball, Craig broke into the major leagues with the Brooklyn Dodgers in 1955 and went 5–3 with a 2.78 ERA in mostly relief work. He would spend seven seasons in the Dodgers organization, moving with the team from Brooklyn to Los Angeles in 1958 before going to the expansion New York Mets in 1962. His body of work with the Dodgers showed a 49–38 record with a 3.73 ERA. In other words, Craig had a winning record before heading to one of the worst teams in baseball history. But once he went to the Mets, the idea of winning became a bad joke, particularly in 1962 when the Mets lost 120 games.

Craig appeared in 42 games with the Mets in 1962—33 were starts—and he posted a 10–24 mark with a 4.51 ERA. The following season he went 5–22 with a 3.78 ERA in 46 appearances (31 starts), including an 18-game losing streak. Ironically for Giants fans, their future manager suffered his worst days as a player at the Polo Grounds, which served as the home field for the Mets during the fledgling franchise's salad days.

Even though Craig lost 46 games in two seasons, he pitched 27 complete games and was generally recognized as the best pitcher on the staff. Pitching purgatory lasted just two seasons, as Craig moved on to St. Louis in 1964. He played a season for the Cardinals and then played for the Cincinnati Reds in 1965 and the Philadelphia Phillies in 1966 before retiring with a career 74–98 record and a 3.83 ERA.

Among his career highlights were starts for the Dodgers in the 1955, 1956, and 1959 World Series. In addition, Craig made two relief appearances for the Cardinals in the 1964 World Series. In World Series competition, Craig posted a 2–2 record, and the teams he played for won three of the four World Series in which they played.

Craig made a smooth transition from player to coaching and managing. First he earned a solid reputation as a pitching coach, which stemmed from his ability to teach the split-finger to the pitchers on his staff. He had stints as the pitching coach for the San Diego Padres and the Houston Astros before he became the manager of the Padres, a role in which he served from 1978 to 1979. After leaving the Padres' manager's post, Craig became the Detroit Tigers' pitching coach from 1980 to 1984 and was given a lot of credit for the Detroit staff's work en route to winning the 1984 World Series.

Craig parlayed his success as the Tigers pitching coach into the Giants' managerial post in 1985. Under Craig, the Giants had five consecutive winning seasons, including a National League West division title in 1987 and the Giants' first National League pennant since 1962 when they captured the crown in 1989 before losing to the Oakland Athletics in the World Series. Craig's Giants experienced losing seasons in 1991 and 1992 before he stepped down from the post at the age of 62 following the 1992 season. Dusty Baker took over for the 1993 season. In eight seasons with the Giants, Craig had a 586–566 record.

46 Attend Giants Fantasy Camp

You could have been a major leaguer if only…

Sound familiar? Well, now that you're a successful professional, you can finally get that tryout for the Giants, sort of. You might have to squint your eyes a little bit in order to feel that the dream of playing in the major leagues for your favorite team, the San Francisco Giants, has come to fruition. But once you are on the turf at Scottsdale Stadium, it becomes easy to buy into the fact you are a major leaguer—at least for a week.

Every January the Giants conduct a fantasy camp at Scottsdale Stadium, where the Giants conduct their spring training operations. All you have to do is fill out a check of close to five grand, and suddenly you're mingling with and playing against former Giants greats as well as others of your ilk who are living the dream just like you.

Men and women, ages 25 and up, are eligible to take part in the camp, regardless of their skill level. The agenda calls for campers to arrive at Phoenix Sky Harbor Airport on Sunday before heading to the Giants' resort in Scottsdale, which will become every camper's home away from home for a week. A welcome reception takes place on Sunday night, allowing campers to mingle with one another while getting to know the former Giants, who will be the campers' coaches during the week.

On Monday morning, though, it's time to get down to business. Campers begin each day with a buffet breakfast before getting shuttled to the ballpark, where they first endure a "kangaroo court" before preparing to take the field for the day's baseball activities, which includes instructions, games against other campers, lunch, a team draft, and practice.

Once teams are selected, the coaches cobble together the pieces to come up with a plan for winning the camp pennant. Tuesday through Friday brings a routine of daily instructions and games played between all of the teams in camp. Everything is well organized to lend an air of being a big leaguer competing for a pennant. The number of former Giants who have participated over the years is great and includes the likes of Hall of Fame first baseman Orlando Cepeda and Cy Young Award–winner Mike McCormick. Just imagine how good the Giants uniform will feel clinging to your body as you grab your bat and glove and head out to the field in Scottsdale. Once on the close-cropped turf, you have the chance to be the one smelling the grass from the inside rather than being on the outside watching the players drift onto the field. Normally, you're the guy on the other side of the fence watching the boys of summer prepare to play games. Now, finally, you are the one inside the arena making the little jokes with your teammates while others on the outside watch from afar and wonder what it feels like to be an insider.

Though many campers learn quickly what it's like to awaken long-dormant muscles in their bodies—and quickly work Advil into their daily regimens—it is a good soreness. And in no way does it prevent the campers from going out after the day's activities have concluded. The camaraderie of joining your fellow campers for a cool one after practices and games is half the fun of being a part of the fantasy. You can rehash the plays that were made—and laugh along with your new friends about the plays that weren't. Many of the former Giants players accompany campers to the after-hours part of the program, allowing you to better know some of your favorite players and hear some of their stories accrued while playing for the Giants.

By the time the week is over, every camper has made a lot of new friends, Giants fans like them or former players. In addition, playing on a major league field will likely give you a new appreciation for what major leaguers do.

Futility in 1985

Every club experiences seasons of futility, those seasons in which having little talent combines with nothing going right to equate to a total disaster. For the San Francisco Giants, that season came in 1985. Not since the team moved from New York to San Francisco had the Giants experienced a season of frustration quite like 1985, nor have they experienced such a season since.

Jim Davenport began the campaign as the manager of this sinking ship, and Roger Craig managed the final 18 games of the season. Unlike most losing seasons, the Giants began 1985 with a 4–3 win over the San Diego Padres at Candlestick Park. Vida Blue got the win in front of 52,714 fans, and the hopes for a promising season were alive, at least for a day. Blue would go on to post an 8–8 mark in 1985, which was well above the standard the rest of the team would set.

After their Opening Day victory, the Giants remained tied for first place for approximately two days before the bottom fell out. The Giants had three wins after five games and then suffered the first of many long losing streaks when they dropped seven straight from April 15 to April 22. After posting a 7–12 mark in April, the Giants found themselves in the basement of the National League West division, three games behind the first-place Los Angeles Dodgers. The Giants kicked off May with a 4–3 loss to the Chicago Cubs and finished the month with a 10–16 mark to continue the pattern that would see the Giants suffer through five more losing months.

By the end of the first half, the Giants had a 33–55 record, including a season-high 10-game losing streak from June 20 to June 30.

They would be shutout 14 times during the season and reached their low on August 25 at Philadelphia's Veterans Stadium when they took a 14–5 shellacking at the hands of the Phillies. The highlight of the season came on June 11 in Atlanta when the Giants took a 5–4 win over the Braves in 18 innings.

When all the smoke cleared on October 6, 1985, and the Giants had finished playing their final game of the season, they stood with a record of 62–100, leaving them 33 games out of first place. The team had extremely poor hitting that saw them finish with a .233 team batting average that produced just 556 runs to finish last in the National League. In attendance, the Giants finished 11th among 12 National League teams, drawing 818,697 fans to Candlestick Park. And no single player had anything that remotely resembled a special season.

Alas, the change to Craig at the end of the season would prove to be the most positive thing accomplished that year. Even though the Giants won just six of the 18 games he managed, the worm would turn the following season. Taking a team composed of many of the same players from 1985, Craig somehow worked what appeared to be a miracle by guiding the Giants to an 83–79 season. Amazingly, that would be the first of five consecutive winning seasons under Craig. For Giants fans, the 1985 season reaffirmed the old adage that you first have to reach bottom before you can climb to the clouds.

48 103 Wins Not Enough

Since the Giants moved from New York to San Francisco, the team has twice won 103 games. In 1962 the team won 103 and went to the World Series. In 1993 they won 103 and went home.

The 1993 Giants went to spring training in February riding a wave of hope. The 1992 squad had endured a losing record in Roger Craig's final season as manager. After Craig stepped down, the Giants hired Dusty Baker to take over for 1993. He brought vitality and enthusiasm to the post. But most of the team's hopes for 1993 derived from the acquisition of Barry Bonds. Bonds had led the Pittsburgh Pirates to the postseason in 1991 and 1992—a season in which he captured his second MVP, before he opted to leave the Pirates via free agency to sign a six-year deal with the Giants worth $43.75 million.

While the Giants had signed perhaps the best player in baseball, the Giants' division had an emerging heavyweight at the top in the Atlanta Braves. The Braves' fortunes were based primarily on starting pitching, and their 1992 staff, which easily was one of the best in baseball, actually improved during the off-season when they signed free agent right-hander Greg Maddux. Aside from Bonds, the Giants suddenly had some pitching, led by the one-two punch of John Burkett and Billy Swift and a bullpen anchored by Rod Beck.

Despite the Giants' roster and the improvements made, the road to a division title clearly ran through Atlanta, which had won the National League pennant the previous two seasons en route to World Series appearances. Burkett started on Opening Day and pitched the team to a 2–1 win over the Cardinals at Busch Stadium in St. Louis, which served as a precursor for the season. Burkett got the win, Bonds had an RBI, and Beck earned a save.

By the end of April, the Giants had a 15–9 record and were tied for first with the Houston Astros; the Braves lagged behind them in third place at 12–13. A six-game winning streak that went from the end of April through early May, coupled with a seven-game winning streak later in the month, fueled an 18–9 stretch, capped off by a 4–3 win over the Braves on May 30 in which a Bonds three-run home run off Tom Glavine had been the difference. The dependable Beck picked up his 13th save of the season the same day, and the Giants held a five-game lead in the National League West.

The Giants followed with a 19–9 June and an 18–8 July, leaving them with a 7½-game lead heading into August, and the team had the sheen of one that could not be caught. But when the Giants slipped slightly in August by going 15–11, the Braves made their move. Included in the losses was a three-game sweep by the Braves at Candlestick Park from August 23 to 25. The month

John Burkett

After a brief major league debut with the Giants in 1987, John Burkett became the ace of their staff after returning to the show in 1990. While he never resembled a turkey on the mound, the right-hander had a great affinity for turkeys—on the bowling lanes, that is. He was an accomplished enough bowler that three consecutive strikes, also known as a "turkey" in bowling parlance, was nothing for him to accomplish.

Burkett's best season in the major leagues came in 1993 when he posted a 22–7 record and 3.65 ERA, helping to fuel a 103-win season for the Orange and Black. Unfortunately for the Giants, they got nudged out of the postseason by the Atlanta Braves, who won 104 games. Burkett continued to pitch well for the Giants until moving to the Florida Marlins in 1995 via free agency. In six seasons with the Giants, Burkett compiled a 67–42 mark with a 3.83 ERA, which included making the All-Star team in 1993.

Burkett moved from the Marlins to the Texas Rangers in a 1996 trade. While pitching for the Rangers, Burkett claimed the organization's first postseason win, which remained the Rangers' only postseason win until the team reached the playoffs in 2010. Burkett earned his second trip to the All-Star Game in 2001 when he played for the Atlanta Braves. Burkett always was a fun guy to have in the clubhouse. While with the Boston Red Sox, he came to be known as "Sheets" among his teammates, since he was the guy who always ran any pools within the Red Sox clubhouse. He retired at the age of 38 after the 2003 season, which saw him post a 12–9 record with the Red Sox. He went 166–136 with a 4.31 ERA in a 15-year major league career. Burkett always loved bowling and excelled at the sport. Today he is a part-time professional bowler and has rolled 12 perfect games in his career.

ended with an 8–2 loss to the Braves in Atlanta that narrowed the Giants' lead to 3½ games.

Unfortunately for the Giants, they lost eight in a row from September 7 to 15 to lose the division lead. After they lost to the Cubs 3–1 on September 15, the Giants trailed the Braves by 3½ games. But the Giants did not quit, winning three of their last five games to fall just short of the catching the Braves. The Giants finished the season with a 103–59 record, while the Braves finished one game ahead, at 104–58.

Bonds won National League Most Valuable Player honors for a season that saw him hit .336 with 46 home runs and 123 RBIs, while Swift went 21–8 with a 2.82 ERA, and Burkett went 22–7 with a 3.65 ERA. And Beck collected 48 saves. It was a remarkable season made even more remarkable by the fact that 103 wins was not good enough to advance to the postseason.

49 Giants Home Run Champions

Since 1909, Giants players have won the National League home run title 24 times, the last of those times coming in 2001 when Barry Bonds set Major League Baseball's single-season home run record. Bonds hit 73 that season to break Mark McGwire's previous record of 70. Oh, how the times had changed from the days when the Giants had their first home run champion. Bonds hit more than 10 times as many home runs to win the title in 2001 than Red Murray did for the Giants when he won the home run title in 1909. Of course, Murray played during the dead-ball era before Babe Ruth truly brought the big fly into fashion, so Murray's seven were plenty to lead the league.

Dave Robertson became the Giants' first two-time home run champion, and he accomplished the feat in back-to-back years, sharing the lead in the National League with 12 dingers in both 1916 and 1917 (he tied Cy Williams in 1916 and Gavvy Cravath in 1917). Four years later, George "High Pockets" Kelly, who played first base for the Giants, almost doubled Robertson's league-leading number when he won the 1921 title with 23 home runs. Kelly would play 11 seasons for the Giants and hit 123 home runs.

Mel Ott won his first National League home run title in 1932 at the age of 23 when he hit 38. "Master Melvin" would go on to win six home run crowns with 35 in 1934, 33 in 1936, 31 in 1937, 36 in 1938, and 30 in 1942. In 1946 Johnny Mize played for the Giants and competed with Ralph Kiner for the National League title, but he broke his toe and ended up hitting 23, which left him one home run short of the Pittsburgh Pirates slugger. However, Mize did not come up short in the two seasons that followed, as he hit 51 in 1947 and 40 in 1948 to lead the league both seasons.

At the age of 23, Willie Mays put a 41–home run season in the books during the Giants' championship run of 1954. A year later the Say Hey Kid would capture his first home run crown by hitting 51 when the Giants still played in New York at the Polo Grounds. Mays would add three additional home run titles after the Giants moved to San Francisco, where the team played in Candlestick Park and hitting home runs become more difficult. Mays led the league with 49 in 1962, 47 in 1964, and 52 in 1965.

Orlando Cepeda had his greatest season as a Giant in 1961 when he set a team record with 142 RBIs. Fueling Cha-Cha's huge RBI total were his league-leading 46 home runs. That would be the only time in Cepeda's career that he led the league in round-trippers.

Willie McCovey hit 44 home runs in 1963 to win his first home run title and became a yearly contender for the crown after that season, though he did not gain another home run title until

Dedicate a Homer to Duane Kuiper

It doesn't matter whether you're playing a game of baseball, Wiffle ball, or slow-pitch softball, the next time you hit a home run, dedicate the blast to Duane Kuiper, the anti–home run king who is a special part of the Giants family.

Kuiper played second base for the Cleveland Indians from 1974 to 1981 before joining the Giants in 1982. While Kuiper had an adequate batting average—he hit .271 for his career—he wasn't the guy you wanted at the plate if you needed a home run. Talk about frustration: in 3,379 major league at-bats, Kuiper hit just one round-tripper. That epic blast came on August 29, 1977. Chicago White Sox pitcher Steve Stone served up the home run, earning both Kuiper and Stone a taste of notoriety, given the fact it proved to be Kuiper's lone home run. He holds the major league record for most career at-bats with just one home run.

While Kuiper's home run earned him some distinction, he established a more positive mark on July 27, 1978, at Yankee Stadium when he hit two bases-loaded triples, which is a feat achieved by only two other major leaguers. Kuiper's 1983 baseball card mocks his prowess with the bat as the photo on the card captures him holding the fat end of a broken bat. He now works as a radio and TV announcer for the Giants, as well as being a part of the duo known as "Kruk and Kuip"—Kruk being former major league pitcher Mike Krukow.

Among Kuiper's more memorable calls—an ironic one given Kuiper's own career—was the one describing Barry Bonds' historic 756th home run that broke Hank Aaron's record. The blast also gave Bonds 755 more home runs than Kuiper.

Since the August 29, 1977, game was nationally broadcast, Kuiper's memorable home run was captured on videotape, and it lives on, appearing on occasion during Giants telecasts.

1968 when he hit 36. The following season, McCovey again led the league with 45 homers en route to winning Most Valuable Player honors. With the Hall of Fame trio of Mays, McCovey, and Cepeda, the Giants captured five straight home run titles from 1961 to 1965, and seven total during the decade of the '60s.

Kevin Mitchell had never hit more than 22 home runs in a season when he exploded with 47 in 1989 to win his only home run title. Bonds' first season with the Giants came in 1993 after he signed a lucrative free agent contract to join the team. He responded to the Giants showing him the money by hitting 46 home runs to lead the league.

Matt Williams won the National League home run title with 43 in 1994, which looked like a normal number for winning a home run crown during an era when a lot of home runs were being hit. What made the number more significant was the fact that Williams accrued his total in just 112 games, as the players went on strike that season, which canceled the last two months of the season as well as that season's World Series.

Buster Posey

Buster Posey has been everything and more than he was cracked up to be when the Giants made him the fifth overall selection of the 2008 Major League Baseball Draft. The Giants catcher had been in the spotlight for a while by the time the Giants brought him into the fold. While going to Lee County High School in Leesburg, Georgia, he was recognized as the Georgia Gatorade Player of the Year, Louisville Slugger State Player of the Year, and an EA Sports All-American in advance of his accepting a baseball scholarship to Florida State University.

Playing shortstop for the Seminoles as a freshman, Posey started all of FSU's games and finished with a .346 average, four home runs, and 48 RBIs to earn recognition as a Louisville Slugger Freshman All-American. The FSU coaching staff opted to move Posey to catcher for his sophomore season, and he continued to thrive, hitting .382 while playing flawlessly behind the plate. By the end of the following season, Posey had become such a good receiver that he was nominated for the Johnny Bench Award, which recognizes the top catcher in college baseball. That same season, he hit .463 with 26 home runs

Giants rookie catcher Buster Posey hits a solo home run off of the Rangers' Darren Oliver in the eighth inning of Game 4 of the 2010 World Series in Arlington, Texas. The blast made it 4–0 Giants, which held up as the final score.

and 93 RBIs en route to winning the Golden Spikes Award, the award given to the best player in amateur baseball.

Posey signed with the Giants after receiving a $6.2 million bonus, and the Giants invited him to spring training in 2009, which is often done with an organization's top pick. Posey did not take the invitation as a chance for the Giants to parade him in front of the media, instead he got to work making an impression on the team's coaching staff, which he did.

He began the season at San Jose, the Giants' Class A affiliate, and by July he had reached Fresno, the Triple A team, which put him in position to be called to the major leagues when Giants starting catcher Bengie Molina went down with an injury. On September 11, 2009, Posey made his major league debut when he struck out in his only at-bat after entering the game as a defensive replacement for Molina. He finished 2009 going 2-for-17, for a .118 batting average.

Making sure they weren't rushing Posey, he began the 2010 season at Fresno and hit .349 in 47 games before getting called up to the Giants on May 29. The following day, Posey went 3-for-4 with three RBIs, and his career was off and running. Playing against the Cincinnati Reds on June 9, he hit his first major league home run against Aaron Harang. He played mostly at first base through June before the Giants traded Bengie Molina to the Texas Rangers on June 30, putting Posey behind the plate. The move did nothing to thwart Posey's offense. He connected for his first career grand slam on July 7 against the Milwaukee Brewers in a game that saw him hit another home run and collect four hits along with six RBIs.

Posey showed just how hot he could be by going through a 10-game stretch in which he hit .514 with 19 hits, six home runs, and 13 RBIs. Included in Posey's torrid July was a 21-game hitting streak, which left him a game shy of tying Willie McCovey's rookie record. Posey took over the Giants' cleanup spot in the order and held his own. His eighth-inning home run against the Chicago Cubs at Wrigley Field on September 21 gave the Giants a 1–0 win, keeping them a half game ahead of the San Diego Padres. On the final day of the season, Posey hit his 18th home run of the season, which also came in the eighth inning, to help lead the Giants to a win over the San Diego Padres and earn the Giants the National League West pennant. Posey hit .305 with 18 home runs and 67 RBIs in his rookie campaign, then finished the season with a bang during the Giants' amazing postseason run, hitting .288 with a home run and five RBIs while flawlessly handling the Giants pitching staff. After the season, he was named the National League Rookie of the Year. No doubt a great career awaits Buster Posey.

Moderately Difficult Giants Trivia

Questions

1. Which player had more home runs wearing a Giants uniform than any other player in team history?
2. Who managed the Giants when they won the 1954 World Series?
3. Who ranks first as the Giants' pitcher with the most career wins in franchise history?
4. Which of these players did not play for the Giants?
   a) Roger Maris
   b) Gaylord Perry
   c) Casey Stengel
   d) Sal Maglie
5. What was the name of the stadium where the Giants first played when they went to San Francisco?
6. What team did the Giants lose to in the 1962 World Series?
7. What future Giants Hall of Famer hit his first career major league home run during the Giants' first game in San Francisco?
8. Who managed the Giants to their first-ever World Series championship?
9. Which Giant struck Dodgers catcher John Roseboro on the head with a baseball bat?
10. Who was "the Count"?

Answers

1. Willie Mays; 2. Leo Durocher; 3. Christy Mathewson; 4. (a) Roger Maris; 5. Seals Stadium; 6. N.Y. Yankees; 7. Orlando Cepeda; 8. John McGraw; 9. Juan Marichal; 10. John Montefusco

51 1997 NLDS

At the close of the 1996 season, the Giants had a 68–94 record to finish last in the National League West division. So the furthest thing from anybody's mind was the idea of winning the division the next season. But the Giants improved by 22 wins and won the division by two games over the second-place Dodgers, which earned the Giants the distinction of becoming just the fourth team in the 20th century to win its division after finishing in the cellar the year before.

Plenty of magic moments occurred along the way. Barry Bonds hit 40 home runs, while Jeff Kent and J.T. Snow hit 29 and 28, respectively. But perhaps the most memorable blow of the season came on September 18. The Giants trailed the Dodgers by one game in the division when the teams met at Candlestick Park. Heading into the bottom of the 12th inning, the score was tied at 5 when Dodgers lefty Mark Guthrie came in to face Brian Johnson, leading off the inning. Johnson then connected for a game-winning homer, giving the Giants a 6–5 win and putting them in a first-place tie with nine games left in the season.

New Giants general manager Brian Sabean had made a bold move prior to the July 31 trade deadline by pulling the trigger on a deal that sent six minor leaguers to the Chicago White Sox in return for veteran pitchers Danny Darwin, Wilson Alvarez, and Roberto Hernandez. Meanwhile, the Giants' playoff opponent would be the upstart Florida Marlins. The Marlins, who finished second to the Atlanta Braves in the National League East, were a wild-card team and, at 92–70, actually had a better record than the Giants, who finished 90–72. Giants fans could only dream about what might have been had the wild-card been in place in 1993 when the Giants won 103 games but finished second to the Braves—and missed the playoffs.

On September 30, Kirk Rueter faced Kevin Brown in Game 1 of the NLDS, which was the first postseason game ever played in Florida. Through six innings, the game remained scoreless until Bill Mueller homered off Brown in the top of the seventh. Charles Johnson answered for the Marlins in the bottom half of the inning to tie the score at 1. But it was Edgar Renteria's bases-loaded single in the bottom of the ninth that gave the Marlins the 2–1 win.

Game 2 once again went down to the wire. This time Moises Alou turned out to be the hero, with a little help from the pitching mound. When Alou singled to center, Barry Bonds fielded it and threw home to try to get Gary Sheffield attempting to score from second. The play might have been close had the ball not hit the mound, killing any chance to nail Sheffield, who scored the winning run.

With the Marlins leading 2–0, the series shifted to San Francisco for Game 3, which was played at 3Com Park at Candlestick Point (formerly Candlestick Park). Jeff Kent put the Giants up 1–0 with a solo home run in the bottom of the fourth. The Giants continued to hold a 1–0 lead through five innings, but Alvarez, the Giants' starter, surrendered a grand slam to Devon White in the sixth to give the Marlins a 6–2 win and a sweep of the best-of-five series. The Marlins went on to defeat the Braves in the NLCS before winning the World Series in seven games over the Cleveland Indians.

52 2000 NLDS

The one-two punch of Barry Bonds and Jeff Kent led the Giants to their second National League West title in four years in 2000. Bonds hit .306 with 49 home runs and 106 RBIs, while Kent hit .334 with 33 home runs and 125 RBIs, which translated to a 97–65 record. Kent won National League MVP honors for his efforts, and manager Dusty Baker came away with his third National League Manager of the Year award.

Winning the division did not come easily, particularly after starting the season with a 3–9 mark—which included a seven-game losing streak. By the end of April, the Giants had righted the ship, finishing the first month of the season with a 10–13 mark. Still, the

Giants appeared to be sleepwalking for the first three months of the season, finishing May and June with 15–12 and 13–13 records, respectively.

Then the team caught fire. In July they posted a 19–8 record before going 19–10 in August and 20–9 in September, including a nine-game winning streak from August 30 to September 7. The Giants posted a 51–26 mark after the All-Star Break, to win the division by 11 games over the second-place Los Angeles Dodgers. In addition, while playing their first season at PacBell Park, the Giants went 55–26 at home, where they drew a franchise-record 3,244,320 fans.

As the Giants did in 1997 after winning their division, they once again opened the playoffs against the National League wild-card winner, which turned out to be the New York Mets. PacBell Park hosted Game 1 of the NLDS on October 4, and the Giants sent Livan Hernandez to the mound. The veteran right-hander gave the Giants a quality start, going 7⅔ innings, while Ellis Burks hit a three-run homer to contribute to the 5–1 win.

Game 2 of the series saw the Giants overcome a 4–1 Mets lead when J.T. Snow hit a three-run homer in the ninth off Mets closer Armando Benitez. Despite the Giants' comeback, the Mets did not get rattled. After Jay Payton's RBI single in the 10th put the Mets up 5–4, veteran left-hander John Franco held the Giants scoreless in the bottom half of the inning to send the series to New York for the third and fourth games.

Shea Stadium hosted Game 3, and fans who liked pitching had to be happy as the Giants and Mets pitchers handcuffed the hitters on both sides to send the game into extra innings tied at 2. New York's Benny Agbayani hit a solo home run in the bottom of the 13th inning to give the Mets a 3–2 victory and put the Giants on the brink of elimination in the best-of-five series.

The Giants seemed to run into destiny in Game 4 when the Mets gave the nod to No. 4 starter Bobby Jones, and he pitched brilliantly. Jeff Kent's leadoff double in the fifth inning would be the only hit the Giants could muster against Jones, who went the distance. Meanwhile, Robin Ventura's two-run homer in the first staked Jones to a 2–0 cushion. That proved to be all he needed as the Mets won 4–0 to eliminate the Giants, who scored just two runs in 22 innings in New York.

1971 NLCS

San Francisco's stars were aging in 1971. Willie Mays was 40, and the Say Hey Kid's best years were clearly behind him. Willie McCovey was 33, and he, too, had seen better days. Juan Marichal, who also turned 33, and Gaylord Perry, at 32, gave the team a long-in-the-tooth look. But having the aging future Hall of Famers combined with the fresh faces of Bobby Bonds and Chris Speier and the guidance of manager Charlie Fox led to a successful season for the Giants.

April belonged to the Giants as they stormed out of the gate to an 18–5 record in the opening month of the season. Included in the opening month's success was a nine-game winning streak from April 11 to 19. After going 19–9 in May, the Giants found themselves atop the National League West by 10½ games over their closest competitors, the Los Angeles Dodgers.

However, the going got tough the rest of the way. The Giants suffered through a 13–15 June and went just 15–14 in July and 14–13 in August before limping home with an 11–16 mark in the final month of the season. Fortunately for the Giants, they had built up a large early lead. In addition, they were fortunate to have the veteran Marichal at his best on the final day of the season, when he pitched a complete-game five-hitter against the Padres in San Diego to lead the Giants to a 5–1 win and protect their one-game

Tito Fuentes

Tito Fuentes hailed from Havana, Cuba, before signing a contract with the Giants as an 18-year-old in 1962. By signing with the Giants, Fuentes became one of the last players to sign with a major league team prior to the United States' embargo against Cuba. Fuentes made his major league debut late in the 1965 season. He showed promise, playing shortstop and second base. He became a Giants regular in 1966, hitting .261.

Unfortunately for Fuentes, his offense fell dramatically in 1967, which earned him a trip back to the minor leagues in 1968. He served the Giants in a utility infield role in 1969, and by 1971 he again was a starter, playing second base for the team. The 1971 season brought a lot of excitement to San Francisco as the Giants fought off the Dodgers to win their first National League West crown. Fuentes rose to the occasion against the Pittsburgh Pirates in Game 1 of the NLCS when he hit a two-run homer that helped lead the Giants to a win, which turned out to be the Giants' lone win in the series.

Fuentes had fielding woes in 1971 and 1972 when he led all National League second basemen in errors, but he bounced back in 1973 by setting a fielding record for second basemen with a .993 fielding percentage. Thirteen seasons after Fuentes set the mark, Ryne Sandberg of the Chicago Cubs broke the record when he fielded to the tune of a .994 percentage in 1986.

The Giants traded Fuentes and Butch Metzger to the San Diego Padres for Derrel Thomas after the 1974 season, and Fuentes played two seasons with the Padres before he became a free agent. He then had stints with the Detroit Tigers—where he hit a career-best .309—and the Oakland Athletics. He retired after the 1978 season. In 1981 Fuentes became a radio announcer for the Giants when they first began having Spanish radio broadcasts. He is now an analyst for the broadcast and remains a popular figure among Giants fans.

lead over the Dodgers. The victory gave Marichal 18 for the season while propelling the Giants into the postseason for the first time since 1962.

The Pittsburgh Pirates were the Giants' opponents in the NLCS. Three wins would put them into the World Series, and the odds seemed to favor them since they owned a 9–3 record against the Pirates during the regular season. Perry started Game 1 for the Giants at Candlestick Park and put forth a solid effort, allowing four runs on nine hits for a complete-game victory in which

McCovey and Tito Fuentes supplied the offense, each hitting a two-run homer in the Giants' 5–4 win.

Game 2 had a much different flavor, as Pittsburgh first baseman Bob Robertson became the surprise hero, hitting three home runs to fuel a 9–4 win and even the series before shifting east to Pittsburgh's Three Rivers Stadium. The Giants felt good about Game 3 since Marichal would get the start. And the Dominican Dandy lived up to the lofty expectations by pitching a four-hitter. Unfortunately for the Giants, two of the hits were home runs by Robertson and Richie Hebner as the Pirates took a 2–1 win.

Game 4 in Pittsburgh had the all the trappings of yet another pitching duel as Perry locked up with Pirates right-hander Steve Blass. The Giants appeared to be in good shape when they chased Blass after just two innings by virtue of a three-run homer by McCovey and a solo shot by Speier, but the Pirates' bats proved equally as effective. Hebner's three-run homer in the second tied the game at 5. In the sixth, the Pirates got busy, scoring four runs on an RBI single by Roberto Clemente and Al Oliver's three-run homer. Meanwhile, the Giants' offense went silent, scoring no additional runs over the final seven innings to take a 9–5 defeat and elimination from the NLCS. Pittsburgh would go on to defeat the Baltimore Orioles in seven games in the World Series.

1987 NLCS

In 1985 the Giants experienced their worst season in San Francisco when they finished at 62–100 (see No. 47, "Futility in 1985"), but once Roger Craig took over the reins as manager of the team late in 1985, the team's fortunes began to change. The Giants jumped to 83–79 in 1986 before arriving to spring training in 1987 aspiring to greater things. And those aspirations would come to fruition. The Giants had an auspicious beginning to their season, winning their first five games and eight of their first 10 en route to a 16–7 start in April to finish the month with a half-game lead in the National League West.

But the Giants experienced losing months in May and June, which prompted the events of July 5, when the Giants traded pitchers Mark Grant, Keith Comstock, and Mark Davis along with third baseman Chris Brown to the Padres for pitchers Dave Dravecky and Craig Lefferts and third baseman Kevin Mitchell. The addition of the new personnel complemented by the likes of Will Clark, who hit .308 with 35 home runs, along with Jeff Leonard, Chili Davis, and Candy Maldonado, proved to be a winning combination.

In July the Giants went 14–13 before going 18–11 in August and 20–10 in September and October to finish at 90–72. They had trailed the Cincinnati Reds by five games on August 5, then went on a 37–17 run to win their first National League West title since 1971, finishing six games in front of the Reds.

The St. Louis Cardinals were the Giants' opponent in the best-of-seven NLCS, and the first two games took place at Busch Stadium in St. Louis. Candy Maldonado's ground-out RBI and a solo home run by Jeffrey Leonard accounted for the Giants' runs in the early part of Game 1. After five innings, the score stood tied at 2 when the Cardinals reached Giants starter Rick Reuschel for three runs. Meanwhile, Cardinals starter Greg Mathews pitched into the eighth before Ken Dayley shut down the Giants in the ninth to preserve the 5–3 Cardinals win.

Dave Dravecky started the second game of the NLCS, and the emerging talents of the Giants left-hander showed when he twirled a complete-game shutout. Will Clark's two-run homer in the third inning gave Dravecky and the Giants all the offense they needed en route to the 5–0 win that tied the series at one game apiece. Also memorable from that game was Leonard's prolonged home run trot, which Cardinals fans deemed hot-dogging, and responded by taunting and booing the Giants outfielder. Game 3 saw a pitching matchup between a pair of left-handers, Atlee Hammaker for the Giants and Joe Magrane for the Cardinals. The Giants' offense came to life early, scoring four runs during the first three innings, which included another Leonard home run. But the Cardinals managed to erase a 4–0 deficit to take a 6–5 win and a 2–1 lead in the series. Home runs by Leonard, Robby Thompson, and Bob Brenly led a 4–2 win at Candlestick and tied the series 2–2.

In Game 5 the Giants scored once in the first and once in the third to tie the game 2–2 before breaking things open with four runs in the bottom of the fourth to take a 6–3 lead. Joe Price took over for Reuschel, who started, and gave the Giants five innings of shutout relief to move to a 3–2 advantage as the series moved back to St. Louis for the final two games.

Cardinals ace John Tudor faced Dravecky in Game 6 at Busch Stadium, and Tudor pitched brilliantly, allowing no runs on six hits in seven innings of work. Jose Oquendo's sacrifice fly provided the only run St. Louis would need, and Todd Worrell closed out the Cardinals' 1–0 victory. Facing elimination, the Cardinals had forced a deciding Game 7 for the following day.

The Giants' Hammaker allowed four runs in the second inning of Game 7, while Danny Cox pitched a complete game for the Cardinals as the Giants lost 6–0, feeling the sting of being close to the World Series only to come up short.

Bay Bridge Series

"Disappointing" would have been the best way to describe the Giants' playoff experiences since the team reached the World Series in 1962. The Giants were denied a chance to play in the World Series in 1971, thanks to the Pittsburgh Pirates, who defeated them in the NLCS. They were denied another chance at the Fall Classic in 1987 when the St. Louis Cardinals erased a 3–2 deficit to take the NLCS in seven games. But 1989 would be different, thanks in large part to the bat work of Will Clark.

With Clark and Kevin Mitchell leading the Giants' offense in 1987 and Rick Reuschel, Don Robinson, and Scott Garrelts anchoring the pitching staff, the Giants won the National League West by a three-game margin over the San Diego Padres. Waiting for them in the NLCS were the Chicago Cubs, who were led by second baseman Ryne Sandberg and right-handers Greg Maddux and Rick Sutcliffe. Clark would prove to be the difference in the series.

In the opener Will the Thrill had six RBIs and finished off the Cubs with a two-run single in the eighth inning of Game 5. In the process, Clark set new NLCS records for average (.650), hits (13), runs (8), total bases (24), and slugging percentage (1.200).

By advancing to the World Series, the Giants earned the right to play the Oakland Athletics in what was heralded as "the Bay Bridge Series." The Athletics appeared to be formidable opponents, boasting of the "Bash Brothers," Jose Canseco and Mark McGwire, and a host of solid pitchers led by Dave Stewart and Mike Moore. Playing the first two games in Oakland, the Giants were beaten 5–0 and 5–1.

When the Series shifted to San Francisco on October 17 for Games 3, 4, and 5, disaster struck the Bay Area as the Loma Prieta earthquake struck at 5:04 PM, just prior to the start of Game 3, which was slated to begin at 5:35 PM. Due to the devastation brought about by the earthquake, which had a 7.1-Richter scale reading, the 60,000 fans at Candlestick Park were evacuated, and the game was canceled. In the aftermath of the earthquake, baseball commissioner Faye Vincent took action by postponing the World Series for five days. After that intermission passed, Vincent opted to

After the devastating Loma Prieta earthquake, the 1989 World Series between the San Francisco Giants and Oakland Athletics resumed for Game 3 at Candlestick Park on October 27. The A's swept the Giants in the Series 4–0.

postpone the game another five days in order to ensure that transmission of the games could take place. San Francisco mayor Art Agnos requested the games not be resumed for a month, a request that was not granted, as Vincent informed Agnos that he might just relocate the World Series to another area if a month's delay was needed.

Once 10 days had passed, the World Series resumed. Sadly for the Giants, the Athletics did not get rusty during the pause between games. In Game 3, the Athletics teed off on Giants pitching, hitting five home runs, including two by Dave Henderson, and one each by Tony Phillips, Carney Lansford, and Canseco, which tied the New York Yankees' World Series record established in 1928. Though the Giants scored four in the ninth inning of Game 3, the Athletics still won the game 13–7.

The Athletics kept their foot on the gas pedal in Game 4. Rickey Henderson led off the game with a home run off Robinson, as they jumped to a 7–0 lead. The Giants managed to score two in the sixth and four in the seventh to cut the Athletics' lead to 8–6, but the A's added a run in the eighth, then held the Giants scoreless over the final two frames to take a 9–6 win in Game 4 to cinch the 1989 World Series.

56 Two Wild-Cards in the World Series

Barry Bonds and Jeff Kent worked together during the 2002 season to provide all the offense the Giants needed. And when all the smoke had cleared from the 162-game season and two rounds of playoffs, the Giants found themselves in the World Series for the third time since the team relocated to San Francisco. Bonds and Kent combined for 83 homers and were complemented by the likes of veterans Benito Santiago, Reggie Sanders, David Bell, and Rich Aurilia. But the Giants were far from being just a slugging team. Pitchers Kurt Rueter, Jason Schmidt, and Russ Ortiz combined for 41 wins, and Robb Nen was on hand to close up shop, accruing 43 saves on the season.

Dusty Baker's troops did not experience a losing month the entire season en route to finishing with a 95–66 record, which left them 2½ games behind the American League West–winning Arizona Diamondbacks. Fortunately, the Giants' record was good enough to claim the wild-card spot in the playoffs.

The Giants played the Atlanta Braves in the Division Series. After falling behind 2–1 in the series, the Giants stormed back in Games 4 and 5 to advance to the Championship Series, where they met the St. Louis Cardinals in a rematch of their 1987 NLCS classic. For Giants fans, the rematch had a much better ending, as

Darren Baker

Darren Baker earned his moment of fame at the age of three while his father, Dusty Baker, tried to lead the Giants to a World Series championship in 2002 as the manager of the Giants. Darren was born on February 11, 1999. Named after former Giants player Darren Lewis, young Darren Baker achieved a quality track record as the Giants' batboy during the 2002 postseason. With Darren helping with the batboy duties, the Giants surged to an 8–0 record.

Darren couldn't work in Game 3 of the World Series after being sidelined with an earache. And the Giants dropped that one to the Angels. Baseball players, being the superstitious lot they are, recognize such things. And the Giants were no different, believing that Darren indeed brought them good luck. Once he returned to the dugout in Game 4, the Giants got back into the win column to tie the World Series at two games each. In Game 5, Darren could again be seen lugging bats that were almost twice his size back to the Giants' dugout, and once again the Giants won.

However, Game 5 would change the fortunes for future batboys based on an incident that occurred, which proved to be humorous and even cute, but could have been disastrous. In the seventh inning, with J.T. Snow on third and David Bell at second with one out, Kenny Lofton hit a triple off the wall in right-center field. Snow scored easily, but as he approached the plate, he noticed Darren wandering toward Lofton's bat in the batter's box. When Snow touched down on the plate, he simultaneously scooped up Darren by his jacket and safely out of the way before Bell followed Snow to score on the play, thereby averting a possible collision at the plate with little Darren. Snow had performed the rescue operation so naturally that viewers had to be really focused on the play to even notice that anything out of the ordinary had happened. Of course, Major League Baseball noticed and failed to see any humor in a play that could have had dire consequences. In the aftermath of the incident, MLB mandated that batboys and batgirls had to be at least 14 years old. But before that rule went into place, Darren did manage to suit up for Games 6 and 7 of the World Series in Anaheim after Giants players agreed as a whole they would keep an eye on the youngster.

Giants manager Dusty Baker (right) watches his three-year-old son, Darren, carry a bat to the dugout, while Barry Bonds (left) and some of the other Giants batboys look on during Game 6 of the World Series against the Anaheim Angels in Anaheim, California, on October 26, 2002.

the Giants powered their way to a trip to the World Series after winning four of five games against the Cardinals.

The Giants' opponent in the World Series would be the Anaheim Angels. The Angels also were a wild-card entry in the playoffs, which meant that for the first time the World Series would have two wild-card teams. The first two games were played in Anaheim, and the California neighbors split, sending the World Series to San Francisco's PacBell Park.

After the Giants lost the third game 10–4, they came back to take Games 4 and 5 by scores of 4–3 and 16–4, respectively, leaving the Giants one win away from their first World Series title since leaving New York. Jeff Kent tied a World Series record in Game 5 by scoring four runs; he also had two home runs and four RBIs. For most of the Series, the Angels pitched around or intentionally walked Bonds.

The final two games were scheduled to be played at Edison Field. And the home crowd grew quiet in Game 6 when the Giants improved their lead to 5–0 after batting in the seventh. But the Angels cut the Giants' lead to 5–3 in the bottom of the inning on Scott Spiezio's three-run homer. The score was the same when the Angels came up to hit in the bottom of the eighth, with the Giants just six outs away from their first World Series title since 1954. Troy Glaus had other ideas, though, as the Angels slugger came through with a deciding two-run double in the eighth to provide the winning margin in a 6–5 Angels victory, forcing a seventh and deciding game.

In Game 7 the Giants took a 1–0 lead in the second inning on Reggie Sanders' sacrifice fly. The Angels answered in the second when Bengie Molina doubled home Spiezio. Garret Anderson added a three-run double in the third inning, and that would be all the runs the Angels needed as their pitching held the Giants scoreless for the final seven innings to clinch the title.

# Jeff Kent

By the time Jeff Kent's career had run its course, he had been a well-traveled and productive major leaguer. He will always hold a spot close to the hearts of Giants fans based on the work he did while wearing the orange and black.

Kent began his career in the Toronto Blue Jays organization after they drafted him out of Cal-Berkeley in the 20th round of the 1989 amateur draft. He became a piece of Blue Jays trivia as they traded him to the Mets on August 27, 1992, for David Cone, who would help the Blue Jays win their first World Series. Kent quickly earned a reputation as a disruptive force inside the clubhouse, and after almost four years in New York, he was shipped to the Indians during the 1996 season. The Indians then traded Kent to the Giants in a deal that saw Matt Williams go to Cleveland. Williams had always been a popular player for the Giants, so the trade was not received well in San Francisco. Giants general manager Brian Sabean caught a great deal of grief about the deal, prompting him to eventually take exception to the criticism by telling the media, "I am not an idiot."

Kent would validate Sabean's contention with his performance on the field for the Giants. In his first season with the Giants, Kent hit .250 with 29 home runs and 121 RBIs, and he continued to thrive in the seasons that followed. Hitting primarily behind Barry Bonds in the lineup, Kent hit .297 with 31 home runs and 128 RBIs in 1998; he batted .290 with 23 home runs and 101 RBIs in 1999 before having his best season in the major leagues in 2000.

Kent's numbers in 2000 were on a par with Bonds, who hit .306 with 49 home runs and 106 RBIs. However, Kent consistently came through with big hits for the Giants all season and finished with a.334 average while smacking 33 home runs and driving in 125 runs. The Kent-Bonds tandem helped lead the Giants to a 97–65 record and a National League West division title. For his efforts, Kent earned National League MVP honors.

Kent's numbers remained steady and he followed his MVP season by hitting .298 with 22 home runs and 106 RBIs in 2001 before helping lead the Giants to the World Series in 2002 when he hit .313 with 37 home runs and 108 RBIs.

Kent became a free agent after the 2002 season, and the Giants did not move to sign him for a couple of reasons. For starters, they had grown disenchanted with Kent after he suffered a broken wrist during spring training. They later discovered he had broken his wrist while riding a motorcycle, which was forbidden in his contract. In addition, Kent and Bonds did not have a good relationship, as evidenced by an episode during the 2002 season

Giants second baseman Jeff Kent connects on a drive during a game against the New York Mets on August 13, 2000, at Shea Stadium. Kent went on to win the NL MVP that year and in 2004 broke the home run record for second baggers with 278 (he finished with 377 for his career).

when Kent pushed Bonds in the dugout. So in 2003 Kent signed a two-year deal worth $19.9 million with the Houston Astros. In six seasons with the Giants, Kent hit .297 and amassed 175 home runs and 689 RBIs.

On October 2, 2004, Kent hit his 278th home run as a second baseman, moving him past Hall of Famer Ryne Sandberg as the all-time home run leader at the position. After two seasons with the Astros, Kent played the final four seasons of his 17-year major league career with the Los Angeles Dodgers. He finished with a .290 career batting average, 377 home runs, and 1,518 RBIs.

58 Giants' First Game in San Francisco

After completing spring training in 1958, the Giants arrived in San Francisco on April 13 facing a new beginning in their new home. The players barely had the chance to unpack their belongings before heading to Seals Stadium the next day to take part in the team's first workout at the venue they would call home for the next two seasons. The Giants' workout took place first since they had a busy agenda afterward, so the freshly relocated and newly anointed *Los Angeles* Dodgers, who were the Giants' opponents, waited until the Giants had finished their workout to conduct their own.

Once the Giants got acclimated to their new digs, they headed toward the Sheraton Palace Hotel for a luncheon, which approximately 1,000 citizens from the San Francisco community attended. Ford Frick, the commissioner of Major League Baseball, echoed sincerity when he told the audience that he felt sad about the Giants moving from the Polo Grounds to Seals Stadium before adding, "But, as commissioner of baseball, I believe this to be the finest move ever made. The progress baseball will make in the next five or 10 years will overshadow all past developments."

Next to speak was Bill Rigney. The Giants manager first introduced all of his players, then he told the crowd, "There they are, ladies and gentlemen, they're your Giants. They'll be out there playing tomorrow. We are figured to finish the season in sixth place, but we don't have that in mind."

In addition to the luncheon, the day's activities included a parade that traveled through San Francisco's financial district and saw parade watchers cover the team in ticker tape and confetti. The estimated crowd that watched the parade went from 125,000 to double that, depending on who did the estimating. After their day of activity, the Giants players finally had a little time to unwind and familiarize themselves with the new city, which was one of the more pleasurable aspects of the move, as the city of San Francisco welcomed the team with open arms. Any players on the team were accorded movie star treatment.

On April 15, the Giants and Dodgers took the field for the major league's first regular season game in California. Both teams were little changed from the squads that had played their previous seasons in Brooklyn and New York. The Dodgers used their usual lineup, save for the addition of Dick Gray at third base, who was a new arrival from St. Paul.

Meanwhile, the Giants had three newcomers to their lineup in Jim Davenport at third base, Orlando Cepeda at first, and Willie Kirkland in right field, each of whom came to the Giants from Minneapolis. A number of baseball dignitaries attended the game, including Frick, National League president Warren Giles, and Mrs. John J. McGraw, the widow of the longtime New York Giants manager.

Don Drysdale started for the Dodgers and was opposed by Ruben Gomez. And it was Gomez who got the Giants' offense started with the team's first hit in San Francisco in the third inning. Davenport drove in the first run with a sacrifice fly in the same inning that saw the Giants take a 2–0 lead. Daryl Spencer hit the first Giants home run in San Francisco in a four-run fourth that included a two-run single by Willie Mays. Cepeda, another future Hall of Famer, hit the first home run of his major league career in the fifth, and Gomez pitched a complete game en route to an 8–0 Giants win.

The major leagues were now in San Francisco and off to a roaring start.

59 Giants Defeat Dodgers in '62 Playoff to Win Pennant

On the final day of the 1962 season, the Giants trailed the Los Angeles Dodgers by one game in the standings. The Giants hosted Houston that Sunday, September 30, at Candlestick Park and could not shake the expansion Colt .45s, heading to the bottom of the eighth tied 1–1. Willie Mays came to the plate to lead off the inning. The Say Hey Kid's bat ran into a pitch from Turk Farrell, resulting in Mays' 47th home run of the season and giving the Giants a crucial 2–1 win. When the Cardinals defeated the Dodgers 1–0 that same day, the Giants and Dodgers finished the season with identical 101–61 records, which brought about a three-game playoff to determine which team would advance to the World Series.

Game 1 took place at Candlestick Park on October 1, and the 32,652 fans watching got to see Billy Pierce carve up the Dodgers with a complete game three-hitter as the Giants won 8–0 to move to within one game of reaching the Fall Classic. Mays had two home runs, while Orlando Cepeda and Jim Davenport had one each to fuel the Giants' offense.

The best-of-three series shifted to Los Angeles and Dodger Stadium the following day. The Giants took a 5–0 lead after batting in the sixth, but the Dodgers answered with seven in the bottom half of the frame to take a 7–5 lead. The Giants tied the game at 7 in the eighth, but Mays got thrown out trying to go from first to third on a single by Ed Bailey, which took some steam out of the rally. In the bottom of the ninth, speedster Maury Wills raced home on a sacrifice fly to score the winning run for the Dodgers in their 8–7 win, bringing an end to the four-hour, 18-minute contest and forcing a deciding third game at Dodger Stadium.

Juan Marichal started Game 3 for the Giants, and the Dodgers managed four runs (only three earned) against him in seven innings to take a 4–2 lead, which they carried into the ninth inning. The Giants' season was three outs away from ending when pinch-hitter Matty Alou singled to start the ninth. Harvey Kuenn's grounder turned into a force-out at second for the first out. Ed Roebuck walked pinch-hitter Willie McCovey, and Ernie Bowman ran for him. Felipe Alou then drew a walk to load the bases for Mays, who hit a ball back through the middle that slammed off Roebuck, allowing Kuenn to score and leaving the bases juiced.

Stan Williams took over for Roebuck, and Orlando Cepeda hit a sacrifice fly to tie the game and send Alou to third. Williams followed by throwing a wild pitch that allowed Mays to get to second before Dodgers manager Walter Alston instructed Williams to intentionally walk Bailey to load the bases. Williams did as instructed by walking Bailey, then walked Davenport—unintentionally—to give the Giants a 5–4 lead. The Giants continued to enjoy good fortune when Dodgers second baseman Larry Burright bobbled Jose Pagan's grounder behind second, allowing Mays to score the sixth run. The Dodgers went quietly in the ninth when Pierce retired the side in order.

After experiencing a 165-game season, the Giants were headed for the World Series for the first time since 1954, but they would lose to the New York Yankees in seven games.

Bonds Breaks McGwire's Record

Barry Bonds took Giants fans for a ride in 2001, and the ride did not stop until the enigmatic slugger had set the single-season record for home runs. Throughout the season, Giants fans brought along rubber chickens to PacBell Park to taunt opposing pitchers who opted to walk Bonds rather than pitch to him and run the risk of his hitting a home run. The rubber chickens did little to curb pitchers intentionally walking him or pitching around him, which was evidenced by the 177 walks Bonds drew in 2001.

When pitchers did give Bonds something to hit, the results made them want to take the rubber chicken solution the next go-round. On Friday, October 5, 2001, Bonds arrived at PacBell Park with 70 home runs on the season, having homered the night before to tie Mark McGwire's single-season home run mark. The 41,730 fans knew all too well that the next ball Bonds put into orbit would establish a new home run record. In the first inning, Bonds stepped to the plate with two outs to face Chan Ho Park. The count moved to 1–0 when Park threw a tailing fastball that Bonds jumped on and drove over the wall in right-center field to break McGwire's mark, which the slugger had just set in 1998. The 1–0 swing was Bond's first since hitting his last, record-tying home run.

When McGwire set the record, he broke Roger Maris' mark of 61 home runs, which had stood since 1961, his pursuit had been a national obsession. Everywhere McGwire had gone, he was cheered loudly. Even opposing players seemed to get carried away when McGwire set the record. On the night he hit his 62nd home run, his own teammates and those from the other team offered congratulations.

Bonds, who despite his many talents, was not the most popular player in the game, did not receive such a reception from the Dodgers, and his pursuit seemed more of one that he and Giants fans experienced together rather than one he and a nation of adoring fans took part in.

After Bonds circled the bases, his teammates mobbed him at home, where he also was met by his 11-year-old son, Nikolai. Fireworks shot into the cool night and *71* sprang to life on the scoreboard. Bonds gave hugs to his wife, daughter, and mother

Notable Team Records

Without question, Barry Bonds holds the most notable Giants team record with the most home runs in a single season. His 73 homers in 2001 is also the major league record and is viewed as the sexiest of all major league records.

However, the Giants do have some other team records that are pretty darn impressive. How about Jack Clark's team record for game-winning RBIs in a season? In 1982 the Giants slugger drove in 21 game-winning runs. Clark's mark is all the more impressive, considering the fact the Giants won 87 games that season, meaning that Clark's game-winning RBIs accounted for almost a quarter of the team's wins.

Christy Mathewson, one of the great pitchers in major league history, holds several team records that are quite amazing, such as: 37 wins in a season; the most seasons with 20 wins (13); the most lifetime shutouts (79); and the most shutouts in a season (11). His 372 career wins as a Giants player won't get broken any time soon.

Talk about rugged, how about Joe "Iron Man" McGinnity? In 1903 he set the Giants' club record for complete games in a season with 44. Jeff Kent set the record for most doubles in a season when he clubbed 49 in 2001, and George Davis set the season record for triples with 27 back in 1893. (Larry Doyle holds the modern team record for triples with 25 in 1911.) Ron Hunt established a single-season record in 1970 when he got hit by a pitch 26 times.

Other than Bonds' home run mark, it's likely that the most difficult mark of his to break is his single-season, major league record for bases on balls, which he set in 2004 when he walked an astounding 232 times.

before he disappeared into the dugout, where he picked up his cell phone and used it to call his father, Bobby Bonds, the former major leaguer.

Bonds' bat held more magic as he homered in his second at-bat that night, another blast off Park that arched high over the wall in right-center field some 402 feet from home plate for his 72nd home run of the season. After the game—which the Giants lost 11–10 to eliminate them from being a part of the postseason—a celebration of Bonds' feat took place on the infield at PacBell. Giants fans chanted Bonds' name as he went to the podium and told the fans, "We've come a long way. We've had our ups and downs. Thank you." Baseball's new single-season home run king then put his face into his hands, and the tears rolled down his face.

In the final game of the season, which took place on Sunday, October 7, Bonds faced Dodgers right-hander Dennis Springer and unloaded his 73rd home run of the season, which is where the single-season home run record stands today.

61 Bonds Breaks Aaron's Record

Did Barry Bonds use performance-enhancing drugs or did he not? That question left a lingering stench in the background as the Giants slugger doggedly pursued Hank Aaron's career home run record of 755.

On August 7, 2007, the Giants hosted the Washington Nationals at AT&T Park. In the fifth inning, Bonds stepped to the plate to face Mike Bacsik. Bonds had already enjoyed some success against the Nationals starter, hitting a double off him in the second inning and adding a single in the third against the left-hander. The crowd of 43,154 fans stood on their feet, watching and hoping that Bonds' compact swing would ignite through the strike zone and produce the home run they all wanted to see. Bonds did not disappoint.

Bacsik delivered a fastball, and Bonds made contact, sending a drive over the wall in right-center field that made baseball history. The moment Bonds hit the ball he knew what he'd done and raised his arms in triumph. Bacsik knew as well, as he put his hand on his cap in frustration, refusing to watch the ball soar off the playing field. The crowd roared at what they had just witnessed. With that one swing, Bonds produced home run No. 756, moving past Aaron to make him the most prolific home run hitter in major league history.

Barry Bonds raises his arms in triumph after hitting home run No. 756 on August 7, 2007, breaking the most coveted record in baseball: Hank Aaron's career mark of 755 home runs. Bonds would finish his career with 762.

The record spoke not only to skill, but also to determination, perseverance, and longevity. Upon touching home plate, Bonds again raised his arms and pointed to the heavens, which was his way of paying homage to his late father, Bobby Bonds. Nikolai, Bonds' 17-year-old son, who served as one of the Giants batboys, met him at home.

Following the homer, a party for 43,154 unfolded. There were fireworks blazing, water cannons spitting, and streamers falling. The Giants assembled near the plate to congratulate Bonds, a sea of men in white uniforms engulfing him. Bonds hugged his family members and waved his helmet to the fans. In a display of class, Aaron looked past the allegations against Bonds to offer congratulations via a videotaped message. Aaron complimented Bonds for his accomplishment and spoke of what a privilege it had been to hold the record since 1974. "I move over and offer my best wishes to Barry and his family on this historical achievement," Aaron said. "My hope today, as it was on that April evening in 1974, is that the achievement of this record will inspire others to chase their own dreams."

Once Aaron's remarks concluded, Bonds took the microphone and talked about his father, prompting a mist to glaze over his eyes. After the ceremony, Bonds made his way to left field, then was called back to the dugout, affording him a curtain call for his grand moment. Commissioner Bud Selig was not in San Francisco for the historic blast, but he called Bonds after the slugger came out of the game and offered his congratulations. He later offered a statement in which he said, "I congratulate Barry Bonds for establishing a new career home run record. Barry's achievement is noteworthy and remarkable." However, Selig also allowed that, "While the issues which have swirled around this record will continue to work themselves toward resolution, today is a day for congratulations on a truly remarkable achievement."

In a postgame news conference, Bonds also weighed in on the subject of his using performance-enhancing substances when he said, "This record is not tainted at all, at all. Period. You guys can say whatever you want." Many have expressed their opinions since that historic August night in 2007, but Bonds remains baseball's all-time home run king.

Matt Williams

When the Giants drafted Matt Williams out of the University of Nevada–Las Vegas with the third pick of the 1986 June amateur draft, they believed they had their shortstop of the future. Williams proved to be a shortstop wrapped in a third baseman's body. He continued to fill out once he first reached the Giants in 1987, and by the time he stood 6'2", 205 pounds, he had made the transformation from being a shortstop to a slick-fielding third baseman with emerging power.

After playing parts of three seasons in the major leagues, Williams had his breakthrough season in 1990 when he hit .277 with 33 home runs and 122 RBIs. From that point on, Williams became a standout member of the Giants and a major force in their lineup. Williams' powerful stroke propelled him to four seasons in which he hit 30 home runs while playing for the Giants, with the most productive of those seasons being an incomplete season in 1994.

The 1994 season became the year that saw the game's players go on strike in August, which would cause the remainder of the season, as well as the World Series, to be canceled. Despite missing approximately a third of the season because of the labor stoppage, Williams finished with 43 home runs and 96 RBIs. Roger Maris' single-season home run mark had not yet been broken. Had there not been a strike, Williams might have been the first to break the

Matt Williams strokes a fly ball to left during a game against the Pirates in 1993 at Three Rivers Stadium in Pittsburgh. He is the only player in major league history to hit a home run for three different teams in the World Series.

record. Instead, Mark McGwire broke the record four years later. Williams finished second in the voting for National League MVP that season.

Williams played one more season for the Giants before getting traded to the Cleveland Indians. Initially, the deal was extremely unpopular in San Francisco since Williams enjoyed great popularity while playing for the Giants, but Jeff Kent was acquired in the deal, which proved to be a good move for the Giants. Williams played in his second World Series while wearing an Indians uniform in 1997.

Prior to the 1998 season, Williams joined the fledgling Arizona Diamondbacks and still holds the team record for RBIs in a season with 142 in 1999; Luis Gonzalez later tied the mark. Playing for the

Diamondbacks enabled Williams to play in his third World Series, earning him the distinction of being one of the few players in baseball history to appear in three Fall Classics with three different teams. In addition, Williams managed a home run for the Giants in the 1989 World Series, homered for the Indians during the 1997 World Series, and finally went deep for the D'backs during the 2001 World Series. He remains the only player in major league history to hit a home run for three different teams in the World Series. Perhaps most important to Williams, the 2001 World Series allowed him to be a part of his first World Series championship.

He retired after the 2003 season. Williams finished his career with a .268 batting average, 378 home runs, and 1,218 RBIs. In 10 seasons with the Giants, Williams hit .264 with 247 homers and 732 RBIs. When the Mitchell Report was released on December 13, 2007, Williams' name could be found among the players mentioned as having allegedly used steroids.

Milestone Victories

In 2005 the Giants became the first franchise in North American professional sports and Major League Baseball history with 10,000 wins. Here's a look at the Giants' milestone victories in club history and when they took place:

Win	Date	Opponent	Site	Score
1	5/1/1883	Boston Beaneaters	Polo Grounds I	7–5
1,000	5/8/1897	Brooklyn Bridegrooms	St. George Grounds	9–5
2,000	8/9/1909	at St. Louis Cardinals	Robison Field	4–3
3,000	9/8/1920 (2)	at Boston Braves	Braves Field	5–1
4,000	5/18/1932	at Cincinnati Reds	Crosley Field	9–3
5,000	6/19/1944	at Brooklyn Dodgers	Ebbets Field	10–2
6,000	4/21/1957	Philadelphia Phillies	Polo Grounds V	2–1
7,000	7/18/1968	at St. Louis Cardinals	Busch Memorial Stadium	3–0
8,000	10/2/1980	at Los Angeles Dodgers	Dodger Stadium	3–2
9,000	7/30/1993	at Colorado Rockies	Mile High Stadium	10–4
10,000	7/14/2005	at Los Angeles Dodgers	Dodger Stadium	4–3

63 Seals Stadium

Seals Stadium came into national prominence when the New York Giants moved to San Francisco in 1958. The newly minted *San Francisco* Giants would call Seals Stadium home for their first two seasons in the City by the Bay. Located at the corner of 16th and Bryant Streets, Seals Stadium opened on April 7, 1931. Nicknamed "Home Plate Mine" since that had been the name on the deed title, Seals Stadium would serve two minor leagues teams upon opening: the San Francisco Seals and the Mission Reds, who were also known as the San Francisco Missions. Because the stadium hosted two teams, Seals Stadium was constructed with three locker rooms: one for the visiting team, one for the Seals, and one for the Reds.

Because the stadium was built to facilitate nighttime baseball, along with the fact that San Francisco does not get a lot of rain during the summers, the Seals elected to not cover the grandstands with a roof. Construction of Seals Stadium—sans roof—cost what a little-used reserve infielder makes in today's game, approximately $600,000. One attraction to the stadium other than baseball was a water tank underneath the grandstand which afforded fans a chance to observe a live seal.

The Seals became the sole tenants of Seals Stadium in 1938 when the Missions relocated to Los Angeles, where they became the Hollywood Stars. The Seals played in the Pacific Coast League, which played a high quality brand of baseball and saw countless stars pass through the league. Among them were all three DiMaggio brothers—Dom, Vince, and Joe—who played at Seals Stadium at one time or another in a Seals uniform.

The stadium initially consisted of an uncovered grandstand stretching from foul pole to foul pole and an uncovered bleacher section in right field. Additional bleacher seating was added in left field when the Giants moved to San Francisco. Since the arrangement was temporary, Seals Stadium kept its name for the two seasons the Giants played their games there while waiting for the construction of Candlestick Park to be completed.

On April 15, 1958, the Giants beat the Dodgers 8–0 at Seals Stadium in the first major league game on the West Coast. During the course of that first game, future Hall of Famer Orlando Cepeda hit his first major league home run in his rookie season with the Giants. In two years of play at Seals Stadium, the Giants attracted more than 2 million fans before Candlestick Park opened in 1960. The final game at Seals Stadium was played on September 20, 1959, when 22,923 watched the Dodgers beat the Giants 8–2.

Seals Stadium, former home of the minor league San Francisco Seals, became the temporary abode of the Giants in 1958–1959. An aerial view shows a packed house for Opening Day against the L.A. Dodgers on April 15, 1958.

Seals Stadium met its demise in November 1959, but part of the stadium continued to live on. A good portion of the stadium's seats, as well as the light stanchions, were put to use at Cheney Stadium in Tacoma, Washington, which is the home of the Tacoma Rainiers. In 2005 Cheney Stadium underwent a facelift, which included new seating. The seats that had once been in use at Seals Stadium were sold for $75 each.

In the years following the razing of Seals Stadium, a White Front discount store was built on the property, and it later became the site for several car dealerships. During the late 1990s, a shopping center was built there. The Safeway grocery store, which is a part of the shopping center, is built directly above where Seals Stadium once stood. Employees of the grocery store like to joke that ghosts of former players can be seen perusing the aisles at the store late at night.

64 Joe McGinnity

Joe McGinnity did not pitch long in the major leagues, but he pitched long enough to be elected to the Baseball Hall of Fame, and his mound work earned him the nickname "Iron Man." McGinnity was a right-handed pitcher who hailed from Illinois and first pitched in the major leagues in 1899. He proved effective from the moment he arrived in the major leagues, posting a 28–16 mark with a 2.68 ERA in his first season with the Baltimore Orioles of the National League.

Despite his success with the Orioles, McGinnity found himself pitching for the Brooklyn Superbas in 1900, where he went 28–8 to help lead the team to the National League pennant. From 1901 to 1902 he pitched for the Baltimore Orioles, which had by then become a member of the fledgling American League. Toward the end of the 1902 season, he followed shortstop/manager John McGraw to the Giants, and it would be with the Giants where the body of his major league work took place.

In 1903 he went 31–20 while making 55 appearances for the Giants. Included in that total were 44 complete games. Certainly his best major league season took place in 1904 with the Giants when he again broke the 30-win barrier by posting a 35–8 record with a 1.61 ERA including 144 strikeouts. Of the 44 starts he made, he completed 38 of them. The following season McGinnity turned 34 and fell off his pace a little, but he still managed to go 21–15 with a 2.87 ERA and 26 complete games in 38 starts. McGinnity's work helped lead the Giants to a National League pennant and a World Series championship.

While an accomplished hurler, McGinnity probably achieved his most lasting fame for performing double duty in 1903. Three times during the same month of that season, McGinnity started both ends of a doubleheader. Even more amazing was the fact he came away from the six starts with six wins and the well-earned moniker of "Iron Man." Later, when asked how he spent his time during the off-season, he quipped, "I'm an iron man. I work in a foundry."

Of course, McGinnity's feat is far more absurd and awe-inspiring given modern baseball's careful handling of pitchers. During McGinnity's time, pitchers threw complete games more times than not, even if they were getting knocked around the ballpark. That does not happen today, given the development of bullpens that house relief pitchers who take over for struggling starting pitchers.

McGinnity truly proved to be an iron man. After posting an 11–7 record in 1908 at the age of 37—McGinnity's seventh season with the Giants—he never pitched in the major leagues again. He went 151–88 with a 2.38 ERA for the Giants and, all told, won 246 games in the majors against 142 losses, with a sterling 2.66 ERA and an astounding 314 complete games in 381 starts.

However, just because he no longer pitched in the major leagues did not mean McGinnity quit pitching. During that period of time, players would play on their way up to the major leagues and they'd play after their major league careers, which is exactly what McGinnity did. The gritty right-hander pitched in professional baseball games until the age of 54. And by the time McGinnity's career had finally reached its end, he had accrued 453 wins as a professional. Four years after quitting the game for good, McGinnity died at the age of 58 in 1929. In 1946 he was elected posthumously to the Baseball Hall of Fame by the Veterans Committee.

65 Try the Basket Catch

Baseball fans gravitated toward Willie Mays. To watch him on any given day in his career was to see perhaps the most physically gifted athlete to ever play the game. But the physical gifts were not all that Mays brought to the party. In addition to playing the game well and having the tools to do so, Mays had a unique sense of style.

When he ran the bases or chased fly balls in the outfield, his hat would fly off, and when he was up to bat, he often took such hard swings that he almost corkscrewed his body into the ground. But the ultimate personification of his style came in the way he routinely made basket catches of fly balls, which was a catch made with the palm of the glove turned upward and the wrist kept close to the body.

Back when baseball was played without gloves, players often caught fly balls in a basket fashion. By doing so, they could hug the ball to their body if they needed to do so. Rabbit Maranville was widely known for employing the basket catch (with a glove) during a career that lasted from 1912 to 1935. While Maranville's method was essentially the same as Mays, the Giants center fielder invented making the basket catch with panache.

By the time Mays reached the major leagues in 1951, virtually every outfielder in the major leagues employed the overhead style that is used today—except Mays. In essence, by using the basket catch, Mays had to be virtually perfect, or else the criticism would have forced a change from the unorthodox to the standard. But close to perfect Mays was, winning 12 Gold Gloves, the award that recognized the best fielder at each position.

To truly appreciate Mays—though it's hard to find a Giants fan who does not—any true Giants fan needs to partake in the exercise of trying the basket catch. First you need a friend capable of hitting you fungos just like the major leaguers catch. Next you need to find an open field where you can run free—and preferably one where nobody can watch you since the art of making the basket catch is not as easily executed as it looks. Some will catch on faster than others. Once you know you are capable of making the catch in said fashion, you must take it to another level, where you can make the catch with the nonchalance of combing your hair. There will be some who simply cannot master this phase because they simply aren't cool enough. Face it, Willie Mays was cool, and not everybody can be that cool.

After at least trying the nonchalance phase comes the graduate work of making the basket catch: take it to a windy venue. Mays spent 15 years shagging fly balls basket style in the swirling winds of San Francisco. So finding a windy setting is a necessity. Just think of any place where the wind is good enough to fly a kite, and it's likely you've found the perfect place to test your mettle making the basket catch.

Chances are the final exercise will convince you that Mays had style, athleticism, and was cool. And he was likely the only guy who could have successfully pulled off making the basket catch without incident.

66 Pig Out at AT&T Park

Sure, the Giants are your team, so you want to see them play in person. But aside from seeing them up close and personal, you want to give your palate a nice day, and AT&T Park is the perfect place to go for eating and drinking while watching the national pastime.

Much of the fun for any trip to San Francisco is based on sampling the many delicacies that can be found in the countless restaurants within the City by the Bay. Nowhere in the minds of most culinary aficionados does the idea of eating ballpark food enter the picture when thinking about making a trip to San Francisco. The Giants obviously took the above concerns to heart when they opened the doors to AT&T Park. Within the confines of the Giants' home ballpark one can find one of the more exquisite menus in the major leagues. This is not your father's ballpark food.

For starters, let's examine the places that are available to whet your whistle. AT&T Park recognizes that those who imbibe like to have choices other than your standard ballpark draft, so plenty of choices are available. If you want a black and tan, try any Murphy's Irish Pub. Three "cable car" bars are located at various locales around the ballpark, and they offer, among other selections, handmade margaritas and Buena Vista–style Irish coffee.

San Francisco is known for wine due to the many wineries and vineyards in the area. So, if wine is in your crosshairs as your beverage of choice while watching your beloved Giants, head to one of the California Wine Carts, where a variety of California wines can be purchased at multiple locations. Of course, a ballpark draft is the standard, and a hard one to beat as the drink of choice at a baseball game. The Giants did not ignore that fact, so naturally, cold beer is offered at many different locations throughout the ballpark.

Among the food favorites is Gilroy Garlic Fry, which also has multiple locations at the park. Their signature garlic fries are of such a finger-licking-good quality that the 10-second rule is routinely violated when even so much as one fry is lost to the ground. Want some comfort food? Try the selections at King Street Carvery, where carved sandwiches heaping with turkey, beef brisket, and pulled pork are available.

If you're looking for something more in line with the unique tastes offered by the Bay Area, there's always the Crazy Crab Wharf. In addition to a superlative crab cocktail, their signature grilled crab sandwich will make you forget about watching the game, and you'll change your focus to having another of these delicious sandwiches.

And for Cowabunga's sake, don't forget the pizza. Portwalk Pizza can be found at multiple locations, and you have the option of cheese or pepperoni. If that's not enough options, you can always go back to the traditional ballpark fare consisting of hot dogs, hamburgers, and french fries. Food just tastes better sitting outdoors at a baseball game, but the food at AT&T Park is especially good. So you want to arrive at the game hungry, and after nine innings you'll want to leave full.

67 Whitey Lockman

While history most remembers what Bobby Thomson did during the Giants' 1951 playoff game with the Brooklyn Dodgers—and deservedly so—the comeback had to begin in order for it to end as it did. And Whitey Lockman played a big role in keeping the momentum going for the Giants until Thomson finished the job with his dramatic three-run homer off Ralph Branca to send the Giants to the World Series.

A native of North Carolina, Lockman signed with the Giants at the age of 17 and arrived to the major leagues in the summer of 1945 shortly before he turned 19. He made the most of his opportunity in 1945 when he hit .341 in 32 games. By 1948 he had earned a spot as an everyday player in the Giants' lineup. Lockman played first base and outfield, but in 1951 he played mostly first base, where he started 119 games, while also starting 34 games in the outfield.

He finished the '51 season with a .282 average, 12 home runs, and 73 RBIs, spending most of the summer hitting in the fifth spot in the order behind Monte Irvin and ahead of the rookie, Willie Mays. Down the stretch Lockman often came up big for the Giants as they somehow managed to hunt down the Dodgers that summer after Brooklyn led New York by 13 games in the standings on August 11. The Giants had displayed such great heart catching the Dodgers that there was no way they were going to quit in the third game of their playoff, even after the Dodgers took what appeared to be a commanding 4–1 lead into the ninth inning.

Don Newcombe started for the Dodgers that day, but he showed signs of tiring when Alvin Dark singled to open the ninth. Don Mueller followed with a single to right field before Monte Irvin popped out in foul territory for the first out of the inning to bring Lockman to the plate. Lockman had already singled off Newcombe earlier in the game when he slapped a double to left field, driving home Dark and sending Mueller to third, where he would break his ankle after awkwardly hitting the bag. That left pinch runner Clint Hartung at third and Lockman at second with Thomson due to hit.

That's when Dodgers manager Chuck Dressen brought in Ralph Branca, and the rest is history. Thomson hit the "Shot Heard Round the World," and the Giants won the pennant with Lockman touching down on home plate with the tying run before Thomson scored the winner.

The Giants traded Lockman to the Cardinals during the 1956 season, but the Cardinals traded him back to the Giants in 1957. Lockman had the distinction of playing for the last collection of Giants to play in New York in 1957 as well as being a part of the first team to play in San Francisco. Lockman's last season with the Giants came in 1958 before he got sold to the Baltimore Orioles. In 13 seasons with the Giants, Lockman hit .281 with 113 home runs and 543 RBIs. He played his last season in the major leagues in 1960 with the Cincinnati Reds. In 15 major league seasons, he had a .279 career batting average with 114 home runs and 563 RBIs.

Lockman became a coach with the Reds after retiring as a player in 1960 and would serve as a coach, a minor league manager, a director of player personnel, and finally as a major league manager, managing the Chicago Cubs from 1972 through 1974.

68 Dusty Rhodes

Talk about a pinch-hitter supreme, how about James Lamar "Dusty" Rhodes? Nobody who followed the national pastime would have argued that point in 1954 when Giants manager Leo Durocher often used Rhodes as a pinch-hitter for Monte Irvin. Rhodes always seemed to come through with the game on the line.

Rhodes arrived to the major leagues in 1952 at the age of 25. Already he had a reputation as player who could flat-out hit, but was a liability in the field. And he was a man who didn't mind having a drink or two. In his rookie season, the left-handed-hitting Rhodes had just 176 at-bats, yet he hit 10 home runs. The following season he had 13 fewer at-bats, but hit 11 homers; in 1954 he hit 15 home runs while also batting .341 in 164 at-bats.

The Giants posted a 97–57 mark in 1954 to reach the World Series, where they met the Cleveland Indians, who had established an American League record by going 111–43 for the season. The heavily favored Indians knew the Giants had a lot of talent—particularly Willie Mays. If Mays had not caught the Indians' attention prior to the start of the World Series, he did so in the eighth inning of Game 1 when he made his famed over-the-shoulder catch of a Vic Wertz drive in deep center field at the Polo Grounds. Meanwhile, the Indians knew who Rhodes was, but they didn't figure he would be the guy to beat them. Think again.

With the score tied at 2 heading into the bottom of the 10th inning, the Giants got two aboard before Durocher sent Rhodes to the plate to pinch hit against Bob Lemon. Rhodes came through by hitting a three-run homer to put the Giants up 1–0 in the Series. In Game 2, Durocher again called on Rhodes to pinch hit in the fifth inning, and he came through with an RBI single to tie the game in the fifth. The Giants manager let Rhodes play the field after his hit, and he delivered a home run in the seventh as the Giants came away with a 3–1 win to go up 2–0 in the Series.

The Series moved to Cleveland for Game 3, and Rhodes again proved to be a thorn in Cleveland's side when he pinch hit in the third and hit a two-run single to help lead the Giants to a 6–2 win. Rhodes was not used in the deciding Game 4, as the Giants took a commanding 7–0 lead before wrapping up the Series with a 7–4 win over the Indians in Cleveland. Rhodes finished the Series with a .667 batting average that included two home runs and seven RBIs to win Most Valuable Player honors.

Rhodes retired in 1959, leaving baseball with a career .253 average and 54 home runs in 1,172 career at-bats accrued over the course of seven seasons. Once out of baseball, Rhodes found work on a friend's tugboat and went on to work there for 25 years. Many were surprised that Rhodes quit playing baseball after just seven seasons, but typical of Rhodes' sense of humor, after being asked why he had done so, he quipped, "After Durocher left the Giants, baseball wasn't fun anymore."

Giants fans will always remember Rhodes for the way he came through during the 1954 World Series, while his teammates remembered his sense of fun. In Durocher's autobiography, *Nice Guys Finish Last*, he noted that Rhodes had probably been the worst-ever major league fielder. But Durocher clearly had a soft spot for Rhodes, as he wrote, "Dusty was the kind of buffoon who kept a club confident and happy. And boy could he hit! Between him and Willie Mays, there was nothing but laughter in our clubhouse."

# Fred Lindstrom

A lucky card game in which the Giants did not even play brought them future Hall of Fame third baseman Fred Lindstrom. Hailing from Chicago, Lindstrom had shown enough talent by the time he attended Lane Technical High School that the Chicago Cubs invited him to a tryout at Wrigley Field at the age of 16. Excited about his opportunity, Lindstrom went through all the drills and came away feeling as though he had impressed the Cubs. That feeling changed after he learned that Cubs manager Bill Killefer chose to play cards in the clubhouse rather than watch the youngster go about his tryout.

Approximately a month later in 1922, Lindstrom signed a contract with the Giants. Lindstrom dropped out of high school prior to his junior year and headed for Toledo to play for the Mud Hens, where he spent the 1923 season. In 1924 the Giants called him to the major leagues at the age of 18. Under manager John McGraw, the Giants claimed the National League pennant in Lindstrom's rookie season, earning a spot in the World Series against the Washington Senators. Lindstrom would be the Giants' third baseman during the Series and did well at the plate, going 10-for-30 (.333) with four RBIs. However, most do not remember what Lindstrom did during that World Series, rather they remember what he did not do.

With the score tied at 3 in the bottom of the 12th inning of Game 7, the Senators had runners on first and second with one out when center fielder Earl McNeely hit a grounder in Lindstrom's direction at third. What should have been a routine out turned into the defining moment of the World Series. The ball took a crazy hop and bounced over Lindstrom's head, which let the winning run score in the form of Muddy Ruel to make the Senators world champions. Earlier in the game, a similar crazy hop had taken place. Afterward, Lindstrom maintained that the ball had simply hit a pebble.

Lindstrom had a love-hate relationship with the feisty McGraw. Personifying this relationship was the time Lindstrom had to be in the hospital after fracturing one of his legs. When McGraw visited his young third baseman, he berated Lindstrom for being careless enough to fracture his leg. Lindstrom told his manager he hoped he broke his leg so he could understand what he was going through. As the story goes, when McGraw left the hospital, a cab hit him and broke his leg. Later, when streaks of gray were noticed on his blond head, someone asked Lindstrom where the gray hair had come from. He explained they had been derived from playing for the constantly barking McGraw.

Lindstrom established a record during a July 25, 1928, double-header when he accrued nine hits. His best season came in 1930 when he hit .379 with 22 home runs and 106 RBIs. He played with the Giants through the 1932 season before being part of a three-team trade that took place on December 12, 1932, and saw him go to the Pittsburgh Pirates. All told, Lindstrom played nine seasons for the Giants, hitting .318 with 91 home runs and 603 RBIs.

After playing two seasons for the Pirates, Lindstrom played for the Cubs in 1935 and finished his career with the Brooklyn Dodgers as a part-time player in 1936 at the age of 30. He finished his career with a .311 batting average, 103 home runs, and 779 RBIs. Lindstrom hit over .300 in seven of his 13 seasons and was inducted into the Baseball Hall of Fame in 1977.

70 Alvin Dark

Giants fans best remember Alvin Dark for starting the ninth-inning rally that put Bobby Thomson at the plate for the most famous home run in Giants history, but he was more than that piece of trivia. Dark proved to be a solid performer for the Giants in his seven seasons while wearing the orange and black. In addition, he served as the team's manager for four seasons, guiding the club to a World Series appearance in 1962.

Hailing from Lake Charles, Louisiana, Dark became a duel-sport star while attending Louisiana State University. Once World War II broke out, he transferred to Southwestern Louisiana Institute, where he continued to play both baseball and football, leading Southwestern Louisiana's football team to an undefeated season in 1943 and to a win in the Oil Bowl on New Year's Day. The NFL's Philadelphia Eagles drafted Dark, but after serving in the military, he returned to the U.S. and opted to sign a contract with the Boston Braves as an amateur free agent in 1946.

Playing shortstop, Dark appeared in 15 games for the Braves in 1946 before returning to the major leagues in 1948 to hit .322 in 137 games for the Braves, helping them win their first pennant since 1914. He also earned National League Rookie of the Year honors for his work during his first full season in the major leagues. Dark fell to .276 in 1949 and ended up getting packaged along with second baseman Eddie Stanky and traded to the Giants for four players prior to the 1950 season.

Giants manager Leo Durocher recognized qualities of leadership in Dark, prompting him to name Dark the team captain in his first season. By 1951 Dark was a National League All-Star and would make the team three out of four seasons from 1951 to 1954. Dark had a stellar 1951 campaign when he hit .303, scoring 114 runs and collecting a National League–leading 41 doubles. And in the final game of the season—the famed Game 3 playoff contest against the Brooklyn Dodgers—Dark led off the bottom of the ninth with the Giants trailing 4–1 and came through with a single. By the time that inning had played out, Thomson had become a household name and the Giants were headed to the World Series to play the New York Yankees.

Dark showcased his competitiveness against the Giants' crosstown rivals in the World Series by hitting .417, which included a three-run homer in the first game. Nevertheless, the Giants lost in six games. He hit 23 home runs in 1953 and followed with 20 in 1954 to become the first National League shortstop to twice hit 20-plus home runs in a season. Dark also continued to perform in the postseason, batting .412 during the Giants' 1954 World Series sweep of the Indians. The Giants traded Dark to the Cardinals in June 1956, leaving him with a .292 average, 98 home runs, and 429 RBIs in seven seasons with the Giants.

After playing with the Cardinals, Dark played for the Chicago Cubs, Philadelphia Phillies, and Milwaukee Braves. He retired after the 1960 season with a .289 career batting average, 126 homers, 757 RBIs, 2,089 hits, and 1,064 runs in 1,828 games played.

Once his playing days were complete, Dark became a manager, serving stints with the Giants, the Kansas City Athletics, Cleveland

Giants shortstop Alvin Dark runs off the field at New York's Polo Grounds after Bobby Thomson hit his "Shot Heard Round the World." Dark, the team's future manager, led off the inning with a single to start the pennant-winning rally.

Indians, Oakland Athletics, and San Diego Padres. All told, he managed 13 seasons and compiled a 994–954 mark. Many feel that Dark would be in the Hall of Fame today had he not missed time due to military service. In a 1969 poll, Giants fans selected Dark as the greatest shortstop in team history.

71

Talk Trash to a Dodgers Fan

Never has there been any love lost between Giants and Dodgers fans. This fact dates back to the Stone Age—or New York, at the very least, when both teams shared the same metropolitan area. If you're a true Giants fan, detesting the Dodgers should be a part of who you are. So if you haven't learned to truly despise Dodgers fans yet, you've got some work to do.

If the Dodgers are playing Iran, you pull for Iran. If the Dodgers have a nice guy playing for them, he still has a character flaw, which is the uniform he's wearing. Finally, if you encounter a Dodgers fan, you must be equipped with the basic tools to break his or her spirit to establish what every Giants fan already knows: the Giants are the best team in the history of the world. For starters, where would you rather play baseball? A congested city like Los Angeles, where you might sit in traffic for an entire afternoon while trying to get to the game? Or a cosmopolitan city like San Francisco, where everyone knows the difference between a chardonnay and a sauvignon blanc, and the climate is the best in the United States? No brainer—point, Giants fan.

Next, which franchise has been the most successful? This one is tricky and must be navigated accordingly. The Dodgers have won six world championships, 22 National League pennants, and made 26 playoff appearances. Meanwhile, the Giants have six world championships, 21 National League pennants, and 23 playoff appearances. So they're more or less even there, give or take a pennant and a few playoff appearances. What you want to stress is the overall record. The Giants' overall mark through the 2010 season was 10,436–8,958 while the Dodgers trailed at

10,135–9,199. So the idea is to concentrate on who has won the most games. In other words, when you get backed into a corner arguing this one, you just say, "Let's talk bottom line here. Which team has more wins?"

Finally, allow the argument to progress to the players who have played for each team, and it's time to whip a little butt. Two words: Willie Mays. The Dodgers have never had a player the likes of Mays—nor have many other teams in baseball history. He's one of the top five players to ever play the game, and the Dodgers have never had a player who could carry the Say Hey Kid's jock.

If they want to move to the argument about pitching greats, most Dodgers fans will think they have you on this one. They'll wheel out Sandy Koufax, and breaking out Koufax's name normally would take the argument against most clubs throughout the history of the game. After all, the famed Dodgers left-hander threw four no-hitters and won 20 games three times. In addition, he once struck out 382 hitters in a season. Nice work, Dodgers fans, Koufax indeed knew how to toe the slab. But, sorry, any Giants fan can trump you with the name Christy Mathewson. While Mathewson only had two no-hitters, he won 30 games four times and won 20-plus games nine times, including 435 complete games in his career. In 12 seasons, Koufax compiled a 165–87 record with a 2.76 ERA. Mathewson went 373–188 with a 2.13 ERA in 17 seasons.

Finally, don't allow any Dodgers fan to roll out Walter Alston on you. Yes, he had a nice run as the Dodgers manager, but come on, can you say John McGraw? Just go to the numbers. Alston's record: 2,040–1,613 in 23 seasons for a .558 winning percentage; McGraw's: 2,763–1,948 in 33 seasons for a .586 winning percentage.

Now that you're armed for bear, go out there and get after those Dodgers fans.

Rube Marquard

Rube Marquard's major league career got off to a less-than-auspicious beginning, but he would overcome his initial problems to become one of the great pitchers in Giants history. Hailing from Cleveland, Marquard pitched around the area and gained enough of a reputation to sign a professional contract. He ended up pitching for Indianapolis, where he pitched a perfect game, won 20 games, and earned the nickname "Rube" for his pitching style that reminded some of Rube Waddell.

The Giants liked what they saw in Marquard and coughed up $11,000 acquire him, though most thought the figure was $13,000, which led to another nickname after he made a lackluster major league debut in 1908: "the $13,000 Lemon." He took the loss in that one game he pitched in for the Giants in 1908. He followed with seasons of 5–13 and 4–4. But in 1911 at the ripe old age of 24, the game began to slow down for Marquard, and everything suddenly clicked into place when he went 24–7 with a 2.50 ERA and 22 complete games. He followed that with seasons of 26–11 in 1912 and 23–10 in 1913, and the Giants won three consecutive National League pennants.

Nicknames seemed to follow Marquard, and he helped create at least one along the way. During the 1911 World Series against the Philadelphia Athletics, Marquard faced Frank Baker in Game 2 and surrendered a game-winning, two-run homer. Baker became known as "Home Run" Baker.

In 1912 Marquard put together a 19-game winning streak that extended from his Opening Day start until July 3. He received a lot

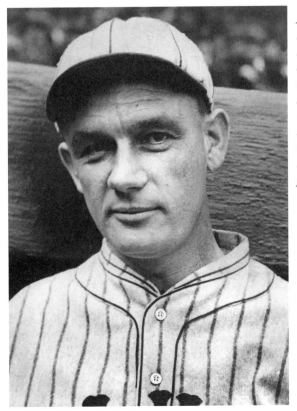

After a rocky start to his career, lefty Rube Marquard compiled a 73–28 record with a 2.52 ERA from 1911 to 1913, to lead his New York Giants to three consecutive National League pennants.

of recognition for his streak and for winning two games in the 1912 World Series, which led to him receiving offers to get into show business. He took part in vaudeville and even made a movie called *19 Straight*. He later acted alongside an actress named Blossom Steeley, and they eventually got married.

Marquard did not overpower hitters with his fastball, though he had a quality heater. Instead he relied on a forkball that he used as a change-up in addition to excellent control. Marquard often was heard to say, "Any hitter can slug the fast ones, but not many can handle the slow ones."

Facing Brooklyn in 1915, Marquard tossed a no-hitter that took just one hour, 16 minutes to complete. Later that season, the then–Brooklyn Robins picked him up off waivers after negotiating a deal in which they paid the Giants $7,500. He had gone 103–76 with a 2.85 ERA in eight seasons with the Giants.

Marquard's worst season came with Brooklyn in 1918 when he went 9–18 to lead the National League in losses, which did not jibe with his 2.64 ERA. The following season, Marquard slid into third base on June 9 and broke his left leg, forcing him to miss the remainder of the season. He managed to get back on the mound in 1920 and did his part to help Brooklyn win the National League pennant by winning 10 games.

Marquard's teams reached the World Series five times during his career, and he posted a mark of 2–5 with a 3.07 ERA in 11 appearances, of which eight were starts. Marquard moved to the Cincinnati Reds in 1921 before spending the final four seasons of his career with the Boston Braves. He retired after the 1925 season at the age of 38. Pitching in parts of 18 major league seasons, Marquard compiled a 201–177 record with a 3.08 ERA. In 1971 he was elected to the Baseball Hall of Fame by the Veterans Committee.

73 Visit the Statues at AT&T Park

For any Giants fan visiting San Francisco, seeing the statues outside of AT&T Park is a must. Since the opening of AT&T Park in 2000, the Giants have dedicated statues to four of the greatest Giants players to ever wear a San Francisco Giants uniform. Noted sculptor William Behrends from North Carolina created each of the statues. His works are acclaimed for the detail and how well he captures actions and traits familiar to the character.

The statue of Willie Mays became the first to be unveiled and was dedicated on March 31, 2000. Of course, the subject for the

Visit the Giants Wall of Fame

Not all of the plaques on the Giants Wall of Fame display Hall of Famers—they are simply Wall of Famers in the minds of the San Francisco Giants family. The Giants unveiled the team's Wall of Fame on September 23, 2008, to honor the greatest players in San Francisco Giants history. Recognized are those retired players whose records rank highest among their teammates on the basis of longevity and achievements. Players who have been honored have played at least nine seasons for the San Francisco Giants, or five seasons with at least one All-Star selection as a Giant. Bronze plaques of these players adorn the wall of AT&T Park along King Street, where all Giants fans can see them. Here is the inaugural class of honorees on the Wall of Fame:

Felipe Alou	Gary Lavelle
Jim Barr	Johnnie Le Master
Rod Beck	Jeffrey Leonard
Vida Blue	Kirt Manwaring
Bob Bolin	Juan Marichal
Jeff Brantley	Willie Mays
Bobby Bonds	Mike McCormick
Bob Brenly	Willie McCovey
John Burkett	Stu Miller
Orlando Cepeda	Greg Minton
Jack Clark	Kevin Mitchell
Will Clark	Randy Moffitt
Jim Davenport	John Montefusco
Chili Davis	Robb Nen
Dick Dietz	Gaylord Perry
Darrell Evans	Rick Reuschel
Tito Fuentes	Kirk Rueter
Scott Garrelts	J.T. Snow
Tom Haller	Chris Speier
Atlee Hammaker	Robby Thompson
Jim Ray Hart	Matt Williams
Mike Krukow	

first statue came as little surprise, given that the address of the San Francisco Giants' new ballpark was 24 Willie Mays Plaza and the most prominent entrance to the park is known as Willie Mays Gate. Located on a palm tree–lined concourse just outside the main entrance at the corner of Third and King Streets is the centerpiece, a nine-foot-tall statue of Mays. The Hall of Fame Giants center fielder is depicted in the aftermath of his powerful swing and gives the impression he is about to explode out of the batter's box to dash around the bases. The statue is cast in bronze and mounted on a white granite base. Behrends called the statue a "labor of love" and said that it took two years to complete, from concept to final product.

A host of dignitaries attended the unveiling of the Mays statue, including Commissioner Bud Selig, Giants icon Bobby Thomson, comedian Bill Cosby, and former Giants managers Charlie Fox and Herman Franks, who both managed Mays.

Barry Bonds, whose father, Bobby, played with Mays in the Giants outfield, called the new PacBell Park "The house they built for Willie." Bonds and Giants second baseman Jeff Kent held the honors of removing the curtain that hid the statue.

Peter Magowan, the Giants' managing general partner, commissioned the statue with the intent of making sure that PacBell Park would be linked to the Giants' illustrious past. Willie McCovey became the next former Giant to be honored with a statue when his was unveiled on May 4, 2003. The statue stands nine feet and is located at the northeast portion of AT&T Park at an area appropriately known as McCovey Point at China Basin Park, which is a popular gathering spot for Giants fans before and after games.

On May 21, 2005, the third statue was unveiled, this one honored Juan Marichal. The nine-foot bronze statue is located at AT&T Park's Lefty O'Doul Plaza and depicts Marichal using his high leg kick. An added caveat to the Marichal unveiling came in a tribute the Giants paid to Marichal and the organization's storied Latin history when the team wore its customary white home uniforms, but rather than "Giants," the letters across the chest of each uniform formed the word "Gigantes," or "Giants" in Spanish.

A statue of Orlando Cepeda was dedicated on September 6, 2008. Like all of the other statues, this one stands nine feet tall. The statue is located at the Second Street entrance to AT&T Park and shows a youthful Cepeda with his familiar smile. "When things like this happen to you, that's when I say to myself, 'Orlando, you're a very lucky person,'" said Cepeda after the unveiling. No, Mr. Cepeda, Giants fans are the ones who feel lucky for having had the opportunity to watch players like you, Mays, McCovey, and Marichal play for their team.

74 The Miracle of Coogan's Bluff

Bobby Thomson's home run off Brooklyn Dodgers reliever Ralph Branca became the exclamation point to the phenomenon known as "the Miracle of Coogan's Bluff." Thomson's historic blast was enabled by a total team effort that began in mid-August.

On August 11, the New York Giants found themselves in dire straits. Most had already conceded the pennant to the hated Brooklyn Dodgers, who held a 13-game lead on the Giants. But apparently nobody told the Giants they were supposed to sack the bats for the season. The Giants had been streaky all season, enduring an 11-game losing streak from April 19 through April 29. At that point, the team stood 10 games under .500, making the rest of the season resemble an exercise in survival rather than a chase for the pennant. Alas, streaks run both ways.

After finishing April with a 3–12 mark, the Giants began to jell. They put together an 18–9 record in May and went 18–11 in June and 17–12 in July. Unfortunately for the Giants, the Dodgers had put together a series of months that made them appear almost inhuman. After going 8–5 in April, the Dodgers went 16–10 in May, 18–10 in June, and 21–7 in July—which included a 10-game winning streak from July 20 to July 31. The Dodgers then won seven of their first 11 games in August, and for all intents and purposes, it appeared they had salted away the National League pennant.

Again, streaks run in both directions. Beginning on August 12, the Giants began to chip away at the Dodgers' lead by sweeping a doubleheader against the Philadelphia Phillies. After defeating the Phillies in the final game of the four-game series on August 13, the Dodgers came to the Polo Grounds, and the Giants beat them 4–2, 3–1, and 2–1 to move to within 9½ games of the Dodgers. Riding the high of sweeping the Dodgers, the Giants traveled to Philadelphia to play three and swept the Phillies to move to within eight games of the lead. So, despite winning nine consecutive games, the distance between the Giants and the Dodgers still seemed insurmountable.

Nevertheless, the Giants pressed on, winning two more against the Cincinnati Reds after returning to the Polo Grounds, followed by a 6–5 win over the St. Louis Cardinals at home before the Chicago Cubs came to town for a four-game set, which the Giants also swept. Suddenly the Giants had won 16 straight to move to within five games of the Dodgers. The Giants finished August with a 20–9 record, but remained seven games behind the Dodgers, who had gone 19–13 in August.

The Dodgers went 14–13 in September, and the Giants continued on their torrid streak by compiling a 20–5 mark in the final month of the season. While the Dodgers finished the season with a 26–22 stretch, the Giants put together one of the most incredible runs in baseball history by winning 37 of their final 44 games of the season, which included a seven-game winning streak to end the season.

The Dodgers actually forced a playoff with the Giants by taking a 14-inning win over the Phillies to finish the season with a 96–58 record, identical to the Giants. A three-game playoff ensued between the Giants and the Dodgers, and that's when Thomson's dramatic hit took place, but that moment would never have been possible had the groundwork not been done in August and September of that season.

# Shooter

Rod Beck didn't have the most talent, but he had heart. When fans looked at Rod Beck, they saw an everyman figure, making "Shooter" one of the biggest fan favorites in club history.

The Oakland Athletics selected Beck in the 13th round of the 1986 major league draft. Two years later, the Athletics traded Beck to the Giants for Charlie Corbell in a minor league deal. While pitching in the minor leagues, the right-hander was converted from a starting pitcher to a reliever. On May 6, 1991, Beck made his major league debut at age 22 against the Montreal Expos and surrendered two earned runs in two innings. But his performance would improve. Beck finished his first stint in the major leagues at 1–1 with a 3.78 ERA in 31 games.

The following season, Beck became the Giants' closer, assuming the duties from Dave Righetti, and he went 3–3 with a 1.76 ERA and 17 saves in 65 games. Included in his work were 87 strikeouts and just 15 walks in 92 innings. In 1993 the Giants had one of the best seasons in team history when they won 103 games and lost just 59. Little wonder that Beck also had his best record when he accrued 48 saves, which included a stretch of 24 straight without a blown opportunity.

After 1993 Beck recorded 28, 33, 35, and 37 saves for the Giants over the next four seasons. In the last of those four years, 1997, the Giants acquired Roberto Hernandez at the trade deadline, and he took over as the team's closer. Still, Beck remained a crowd favorite and put forth one of the gutsiest perform team history at the end of the 1997 season.

On September 18, the Giants were playing the Dodgers at Candlestick Park when the game moved into the 10th inning tied at 5 when Beck entered the game. Three days earlier, he had blown a save, and clearly the season had worn him down to where he did not have his best stuff, leaving him to pitch with smoke and mirrors and a lot of guile. Immediately he got into trouble by giving up singles to Mike Piazza, Eric Karros, and Raul Mondesi, which earned a mound visit. Dusty Baker left the game in Beck's hands,

Difficult Giants Trivia

Questions

1. Who was on deck for the Giants when Bobby Thomson hit his "Shot Heard Round the World" that defeated the Dodgers in the 1951 National League playoff game?
2. Which Giants pitcher holds the team record—after the team moved to San Francisco—for most consecutive scoreless innings with 40?
3. In what year did the Giants spend their final season in New York?
4. Which team did Fred Merkle's famed "boner" come against?
5. What former Giants relief pitcher was known as "Shooter"?
6. What city did the Giants almost relocate to in the 1990s after the team was sold?
7. Who did the Giants trade to acquire pitcher Christy Mathewson?
8. What Giants player broke his ankle sliding into third base just prior to Bobby Thomson hitting his game-ending three-run homer in the third game of the Giants' 1951 playoff with the Dodgers?
9. Which team did Leo Durocher manage prior to becoming the manager of the Giants?
10. Which Cleveland Indians player hit the ball that Willie Mays caught in Game 1 of the 1954 World Series, which came to be known as "the Catch"?

Answers

1. Willie Mays; 2. Gaylord Perry; 3. 1957; 4. Chicago Cubs; 5. Rod Beck; 6. St. Petersburg, Florida; 7. Amos Rusie; 8. Don Mueller; 9. Brooklyn Dodgers; 10. Vic Wertz

and Rod struck out Todd Zeile looking, then retired pinch-hitter Eddie Murray on an inning-ending double play. Two innings later, Beck earned the decision when Brian Johnson hit a walk-off home run for a 6–5 Giants win.

Beck took the free agent route prior to the 1998 season and ended up with the Cubs for two seasons. In seven seasons pitching for the Giants, Beck went 21–28 with a 2.97 ERA and 199 saves. In his first season with the Cubs, Beck posted a career-high 51 saves, the last of which he earned during a one-game playoff against the Giants at Wrigley Field to determine that year's wild-card entry, which the Cubs won 5–3. He followed that season with just seven saves in 1999 before being traded to the Red Sox. He pitched several seasons for the Red Sox and San Diego Padres before retiring after the 2004 season.

In 13 seasons in the major leagues, Beck went 38–45 with a 3.30 ERA and 286 saves. On June 23, 2007, Beck died at his home in Phoenix, Arizona, from an unknown cause.

Sal Maglie

Sal Maglie earned his notorious nickname, "the Barber," because opposing hitters never wanted to dig in too close when facing him for fear of getting a close shave. Whenever Maglie pitched, he believed he owned the plate and batters were simply visitors to his home. As he liked to say, "When I'm pitching, the plate is mine."

A native of Niagara Falls, New York, Maglie first reached the major leagues in 1945 with the Giants when he went 5–4 with a 2.35 ERA. After that season, the Mexican League began to court major leaguers, and Maglie bit on an offer despite warnings from

Major League Baseball about repercussions. Unfortunately for Maglie and the Giants, baseball commissioner Happy Chandler followed through on those warnings and banned Maglie from organized baseball. By 1949, the ban had been lifted, but Maglie opted to play elsewhere for more money than the Giants would pay him. However, he did return to the major leagues and the Giants in 1950, and he quickly showed the Giants what they had been missing while he played south of the border.

Making his return at the age of 33, Maglie initially worked in the bullpen before getting into the starting rotation, going 18–4 with a 2.71 ERA in 1950. Maglie followed in 1951 with his best season in the major leagues when he posted a 23–6 mark with a 2.93 ERA, which the Giants needed while hunting down the Dodgers and finally catching them to force a three-game playoff to determine which team would go to the World Series.

Maglie started the third and deciding playoff game against the Dodgers and pitched eight innings in the game that saw Bobby Thomson hit the "Shot Heard Round the World." The Giants went on to play the New York Yankees—and lose—in the World Series. Maglie took the loss in his only start.

Maglie's teammate on the Giants, Alvin Dark, wrote of Maglie in his 1980 book *When in Doubt, Fire the Manager*, "He [Sal Maglie] is the only man I've ever seen pitch a shutout on a day when he had absolutely nothing. Pitchers have those days, Maglie got by on meanness." Maglie pitched three and a half more seasons for the Giants, posting a 14–6 mark with a 3.26 ERA in 1954 when the Giants won the National League pennant before playing the Cleveland Indians in the World Series. He had one start but did not get a decision as the Giants swept the Indians.

The Giants put Maglie on waivers during the 1955 season. In seven seasons with the team, he compiled a 95–42 record with a 3.13 ERA in 221 games. Maglie went from the Giants to the Indians in 1955 and would have stints with the Dodgers, Yankees, and Cardinals before retiring after the 1958 season. He had the distinction of playing for all three New York major league teams.

Maglie did have some memorable moments and seasons following his departure from the Giants. In 1956 he went 13–5 with a 2.87 ERA for the Dodgers—which included a no-hitter—and was so impressive that he finished second to teammate Don Newcombe for the Cy Young Award and Most Valuable Player honors. Maglie made two starts in the 1956 World Series, winning one and losing the other, as he was the opposing pitcher when Don Larsen pitched the only perfect game in World Series history. Maglie was a two-time National League All-Star, once led the league in ERA, once led the league in wins, and once led the league in shutouts. He finished his career with a very impressive 119–62 mark with a 3.15 ERA. After he retired, Maglie coached, serving on the Boston Red Sox staff as well as the Seattle Pilots.

77 Mays Breaks Ott's HR Mark

Back when home runs were the real deal and had not been tainted by the local pharmacist, hitting 500 home runs was a phenomenal accomplishment. When the 1966 season started, Babe Ruth owned the career mark for home runs with 714, while Giants great Mel Ott owned the National League record with 511 home runs.

Willie Mays hit his first home run at the age of 20 against future Hall of Famer Warren Spahn. Fifteen years later, Mays began the 1966 season with 505 home runs, putting Ott directly in his crosshairs. On April 24, Mays had stepped to the plate in the eighth inning to face Jim Owens of the Houston Astros in a game at the Astrodome. He greeted the Houston reliever by slamming his sixth home run of the season. The blast was the 511th home run of his career. Mays was now tied with Ott, who had hit the final home run of his illustrious career in 1946. Just one more home run and Mays would become the National League's all-time home run leader.

But the record breaker did not come easily. Mays began to press, getting three hits in his next 21 at-bats, watching his batting average go into a free fall from .348 to .284, as he went seven games without hitting a home run. The Dodgers came to Candlestick Park on May 4, and Claude Osteen started for Los Angeles. The left-hander carved up Mays in his first two at-bats, retiring him both times on strikeouts. Joe Gibbon was pitching well for the Giants, who led 4–1 when they went to bat in the bottom of the fifth. After Osteen retired Jim Davenport and Ollie Brown, Mays stepped to the plate for his third at-bat. Osteen delivered his first pitch, a change-up, and Mays swung. Suddenly, Candlestick Park erupted as the 28,220 fans saw what they had come to see—Mays had connected and sent the ball sailing out of park.

"It was a bad pitch, and the minute I threw it, I knew it was going out," Osteen said. "That was just where he likes the ball to be." To put Mays' home run in proper perspective, consider that not only had no other player in the history of the National League hit that many home runs at the time, but just three other players in the history of the game—all American Leaguers—had accrued more home runs during their major league careers: Ted Williams (521), Jimmie Foxx (534), and Babe Ruth (714).

Only after Mays had hit his historic home run would he admit to feeling some pressure about surpassing Ott. "You have to have pressures when everybody is wondering when you'll hit that home run," Mays said. "I've been a little excited and not hitting at all.... The last 10 days I've been trying for the home run to get this over. Now I want to go back to playing ball.... I would like to concentrate now on my batting average. But I'm not going to stop swinging. If ever I come close to another record, I guess it will be the same."

Not only had Mays served up a historic home run with his 512th, he also helped the Giants increase their lead en route to a 6–1 win, which would become the fourth consecutive win of what would develop into a 12-game winning streak.

78 Brian Johnson Sinks Dodgers

Little-known catcher Brian Johnson bounced around the major leagues for eight seasons and never played that much. Most fans didn't even know he was on the team. But fate found him when he wore the orange and black, and the native of Oakland, California, gave the Giants one of the team's biggest hits since moving to San Francisco from New York back in 1958.

The Yankees drafted Johnson out of Stanford University in 1989, and he first reached the major leagues with the San Diego Padres in 1994. After three seasons in San Diego, which saw him play in 186 games, he moved to the Tigers for half a season in 1997 before heading west to the Giants via a trade that sent Marcus Jensen to the Tigers on July 16, 1997. After finishing in last place in 1996, the Giants found themselves in the thick of the pennant race in 1997. But the Dodgers made their push in early September to claim first place and took a two-game lead in a two-game series between the teams at 3Com Park beginning on September 17.

The Giants took the first game of the series 2–1 to move to within a game of tying the Dodgers for the lead. 3Com Park felt like heaven as the teams prepared to play the second game of the series on a sun-baked Thursday afternoon when the wind whispered rather than howled for a change, and 52,188 fans showed for the contest. Knuckleballer Tom Candiotti started for the Dodgers and was opposed by Terry Mulholland for the Giants. Otis Nixon's solo home run in the first put the Dodgers up 1–0, and Glenallen Hill's RBI single in the first made it a 1–1 tie. J.T. Snow added a solo home run in the bottom of the fourth to put the Giants up 2–1 in advance of Barry Bonds' three-run homer in the fifth that gave the Giants a 5–1 lead.

But the Dodgers scored two in the sixth and two in the seventh to tie the score at 5, and that's where the score stood after nine innings. The Giants managed to escape the 10th despite the Dodgers loading the bases with no outs. Popular reliever Rod Beck then rose to the occasion by striking out Todd Zeile and getting Eddie Murray to hit into an inning-ending double play. 3Com Park felt electric as none of the crowd appeared to make an early departure for home, and the noise grew increasingly loud as the suspense increased.

Johnson led off the bottom of the 12th with two hits under his belt ready to face Mark Guthrie. The veteran left-hander delivered a fastball to the right-handed hitting Johnson, and he connected, sending a drive toward the fence in left field. Would the ball get out of the park? Ultimately, the wind would make that decision. Innings earlier, a drive such as Johnson's would have stayed inside the park after hitting the wall of wind that acted like a force field. Fortunately for the Giants, the wind had changed its disposition, and Johnson's drive finished on the other side of the fence to give the Giants a 6–5 win in the four-hour, eight-minute contest.

Once Johnson fought through the mob of his teammates to touch home plate, the Giants were tied for first place with the Dodgers. The Giants won six of their last nine games to win the National League West division, earning their first postseason spot in eight years.

79 Learn to Hate the Dodgers

Former Giants slugger Dave Kingman once noted that acquiring a distaste for the Dodgers was a mandatory exercise for those with the Giants. "It was engrained in you as soon as you came up [to the big leagues]," Kingman said. "It was such an intense rivalry. We were always getting into fights. Guys would throw at each other, and the benches would empty."

Thus, if you profess to be a true Giants fan, learning to hate the Dodgers is a must. The Giants-Dodgers rivalry remains one of the most heated rivalries in sports, as well as one of the longest-standing. New York City had many professional baseball teams in the 1880s before two teams emerged, with the Giants representing the National League and the Dodgers (then and until 1932 known under a succession of aliases, including the Atlantics, Grays, Bridegrooms, Grooms, Superbas, and Robins) the American Association. In what is recognized as one of the earliest "world's championship" series, the Giants beat the Dodgers six games to three in 1889. Following that championship, the Dodgers moved to the National League in 1890.

The Giants and Dodgers have always been geographic rivals—while in the New York City area and today in California—but the identities of the fans of the teams has added to the rivalry over the years. Before moving to the West Coast, Giants fans were viewed as upper-class Manhattanites while the Dodgers fans were a blue-collar group who felt that Brooklyn was their own country and the Dodgers their army.

Personalities played a role in the early rivalry, as well. John McGraw, the manager of the Giants, and Charlie Ebbets, the owner of the Dodgers, carried on a personal battle that helped fuel the bad blood between the two teams. Over the years, the rivalry has remained intense. In 1912 an Opening Day crowd grew so unruly that the game got called after six innings, with the Giants taking an 18–3 win. McGraw also had a celebrated feud with Wilbert Robinson, Brooklyn's manager. Robinson had once been a friend of McGraw's and a coach on the Giants staff before McGraw fired him. Included in their feud was the October 3, 1916, game when McGraw left the Brooklyn victory early. Brooklyn clinched the pennant that day, and Robinson felt that McGraw's early departure had been caused by his jealousy of Robinson's success and that McGraw had "pissed on my pennant," according to Robinson. When Ebbets died on April 18, 1925, the date coincided with a Giants-Dodgers contest at Ebbets Field. The game played on because Ebbets would not have wanted to cancel a Giants-Dodgers game.

Jackie Robinson personified just how much the teams did not like each other when he opted to retire rather than report to the Giants after the Dodgers traded him to their rival after the 1957 season.

When the teams moved to San Francisco and Los Angeles, the animosities moved with them. And while the differences changed shape, they remained great. Los Angeles was Hollywood glitz, while San Francisco was deemed the more cosmopolitan city, overflowing with culture. Both of the California cities competed for business.

The most notorious incident between the two teams took place in 1965 at Candlestick Park when Giants pitcher Juan Marichal clubbed Dodgers catcher John Roseboro on the head with a base-ball bat during a game on August 22 (see No. 26, "John Roseboro Incident").

The Giants and Dodgers have met more times than any two teams in major league history, with the Giants ranking first in number of all-time wins and the Dodgers ranking third. Prior to

S.F. Giants–L.A. Dodgers Pennant Drama

Obviously, the 1951 season brought the most memorable finish to a pennant race between the Giants and their hated rivals, the Brooklyn Dodgers, when the Giants erased a 13½-game deficit to force a playoff that the Giants won on the "Shot Heard Round the World."

But that was New York. Here are some of the other more memorable outcomes for pennant races determined between the two teams after they moved to San Francisco and Los Angeles.

The Giants had the National League pennant wrapped up in 1959, or so they thought. Unfortunately for the Giants, the Dodgers swept a three-game series against the Giants by first taking a doubleheader on September 19 before taking the final game on September 20.

The Giants answered in 1962 when they caught the Dodgers to force a three-game playoff at the end of the season. The Giants won Game 3 of the playoff by scoring four runs in the ninth inning. Ouch! How did that one feel, Dodgers fans?

In 1965 the Dodgers countered a 14-game winning streak by the Giants with a 13-game winning streak of their own to beat the Giants by two games and claim the National League pennant.

The Dodgers felt like they had the pennant in 1971 after charging back from 8½ games behind the Giants to move to within one game of the first-place Giants with one game left in the season. But the Giants won on the final day to trump the Dodgers' win that same day, earning the Giants their first National League West title.

In 1982 the Giants were eliminated but managed to ruin the Dodgers' pennant hopes. The Dodgers entered the final weekend of the 1982 season a game behind the Atlanta Braves. While the Dodgers beat the Giants in the first two games of their weekend series, the Braves won the first two games of their weekend series against the San Diego Padres. But when the Braves lost to the Padres on the final day of the season, the Giants ruined the Dodgers' party by winning the final game of the season, making the Braves the National League West champions. And guess what? The Giants celebrated as if they had won the pennant themselves.

both teams relocating to the West Coast, the Giants held a 722–671 advantage against their rival in 68 seasons. Since both teams moved to California, the Dodgers hold a slight edge in wins against the Giants.

Ironically, the rivals managed to become partners in negotiating their exodus from New York to California since neither team would have been granted permission to relocate to California had either team declined to come. Talk about odd bedfellows.

J.T. Snow

J.T. Snow had been around the block by the time the Angels traded him to the Giants in 1996. He had already played for the Yankees and the Angels, but San Francisco would become home for the slick-fielding first baseman.

The son of former NFL receiver Jack Snow, J.T. played basketball, football, and baseball at Los Alamitos High School in Los Alamitos, California. He attended the University of Arizona, where he played baseball for three seasons before the New York Yankees selected him in the fifth round of the 1989 draft. By 1992, at age 24, Snow got his first taste of the major leagues, playing in seven games for the Yankees. Typical of the Yankees during the 1980s and early 1990s, when they were prone to trade their young talent, they packaged Snow with Jerry Nielsen and Russ Springer and shipped them to the California Angels for Jim Abbott.

While playing first base for the Angels from 1993 to 1996, Snow won two Gold Gloves—more would follow. Not only could he make the plays, he looked smooth while doing so and had terrific range. Angels infielders made fewer errors due to Snow's ability to dig balls out of the dirt. But he never quite became the hitter everyone forecast he would become.

Following the 1996 season, the Angels traded Snow to the Giants for left-hander Allen Watson and minor league pitcher Fausto Macey. Snow had a productive first season for the Giants when he hit .281 with 28 home runs and 104 RBIs. A subpar season followed in 1998 before Snow made a change. He had spent his first six seasons in the major leagues as a switch-hitter. Beginning in 1999 he hit exclusively left-handed, and his numbers improved following the switch, as he hit .274 with 24 home runs and 98 RBIs that season. A memorable moment from that year came when Snow executed a gem in the field on June 26, 1999. That's the game when Snow reverted to Little League days by employing the hidden-ball trick to tag out Carlos Pérez of the Dodgers, which would be the last time in the 20th century that the old ploy would be successfully used in a major league game.

Snow had another good season with the bat in 2000 when he hit .284 with 19 homers and 96 RBIs. He had a clutch hit in the 2000 NLDS when he hit a three-run pinch-hit homer against Mets reliever Armando Benitez to tie the score at 4. But the Mets ended up winning in the 10th inning.

Snow then endured a period in which he encountered numerous injuries. He finally emerged from the storm in 2004 when he hit .327 with 12 home runs and 60 RBIs. He played one more season with the Giants before spending the 2006 season playing for the Red Sox. He did not play in 2007 and returned to the Giants in 2008 when the team signed him to a one-day contract. He took the field on September 27 and was replaced prior to the first pitch, which allowed him to retire in a Giants uniform.

In 16 major league seasons, Snow hit .268 with 189 home runs and 877 RBIs, most of which was accomplished during his 10 seasons with the Giants when he hit .273 with 124 home runs and 615 RBIs. He won six Gold Glove awards at first base, four of which came with the Giants in consecutive seasons, 1997 to 2000.

Eddie Stanky

In terms of his 11-year major league career, the time Eddie Stanky spent with the Giants proved to be just a whisper. Yet his days wearing the orange and black were memorable. Leo Durocher, who managed the Giants during Stanky's tenure with the team from 1950 to 1951, once commented on Stanky's ability by saying, "He can't hit, can't run, can't field. He's no nice guy.... All the little S.O.B. can do is win."

Given that characterization, Stanky's nickname, "the Brat," came as no surprise. Among Stanky's hijinks was an innovative approach toward arriving to home plate faster on a sacrifice fly. Rather than stand on the bag and wait for the fielder to catch the baseball, he would go out to left field and get a running start toward third base. He timed his sprint toward the base so he could touch the bag right after the ball was caught so he would be in full stride sprinting for home when the fielder made his throw. Such a move eventually was outlawed, but the fact he thought up such a move served as a testament to his guile.

In addition, Stanky also employed what became known as the "Stanky maneuver," which would see him jump up and down behind the pitcher, waving his arms and doing whatever he could to distract opposing hitters. No doubt such antics encouraged future generations of basketball fans to employ similar methods when the opposing team's players went to the free-throw line.

A native of Philadelphia, the feisty Stanky stood just 5′8″, 170 pounds. He first played in the major leagues for the Cubs in 1943. Though he played shortstop and third base, he played mostly second throughout his career. After spending one more season in Chicago, the Cubs traded Stanky to the Brooklyn Dodgers for Bob Chipman during the 1944 season. He played with the Dodgers from 1944 to 1947. During that period, he played for the pennant-winning Dodgers team of 1947 while earning a reputation as a master at drawing a walk.

In 1945 Stanky played in 153 games and drew an incredible 148 walks. He followed with 137 in 1946 and 103 in 1947. His 137 walks in 1946 combined with a .273 batting average allowed him to lead the National League with a .436 on-base percentage.

Stanky spent the 1948 and 1949 seasons with the Boston Braves before the Braves traded Stanky and Alvin Dark to the Giants for four players. That trade proved to be one of the most fortuitous in Giants history, as both Stanky and Dark brought a spark to the club managed by Durocher. Stanky put together his best season in the major leagues in his first season with the Giants in 1950 when he posted a .300 average while drawing 144 walks for a .460 on-base percentage. During that same season, he drew a walk in seven consecutive plate appearances to tie a major league record.

Stanky helped lead the Giants to the 1951 National League pennant when he walked 127 times. In the World Series against the Yankees, Stanky managed to get under the skin of Yankees short-stop Phil Rizzuto by kicking the ball loose on a play at second base. Nevertheless, the Yankees defeated the Giants in that Series. All told, Stanky played in three World Series from 1947 to 1951 with three different teams.

Following the 1951 season, the Giants traded Stanky to the St. Louis Cardinals, where he became the team's player/manager. Stanky went on to manage the Cardinals for four seasons. He later managed the Chicago White Sox for three seasons and served an abbreviated stint as the Texas Rangers manager for one game in 1977.

82 Giants Rookies of the Year

The Giants have had six players honored as Rookie of the Year since the award was established. The Chicago chapter of the Baseball Writers Association of America (BBWAA) introduced the award in 1940, picking an informal winner from 1940 to 1946. In 1947 the award became an officially recognized honor, and the Dodgers' Jackie Robinson won the initial award. Only one award was given out for both leagues in 1947 and 1948. Since then, the American and National leagues have both had a player recognized as Rookie of the Year.

At one time the qualifications for being classified a rookie fell to the individual BBWAA voters. That changed in 1957 when parameters were established that tabbed a player a rookie if he had less than 45 innings pitched or 75 at-bats in any prior major league season. Later these guidelines were changed to 45 innings pitched and 90 at-bats, or 45 days on a major league roster prior to September 1 of the previous year. In 1971 the parameters were expanded to 50 innings pitched and 130 at-bats, or 45 days on the active roster of a major league team (which excludes time spent on the disabled list as well as military service). Beginning in 1980 voters selected three players on their ballots. Once the ballots are collected, the tally begins with first-place votes receiving five points, second-place three, and third place one. The player with the highest total of points receives the award.

When the award first came into being, it was called the J. Louis Comiskey Memorial Award in honor of the Chicago White Sox owner. In 1987 the award became the Jackie Robinson Award to coincide with the 40th anniversary of Robinson's breaking baseball's color barrier.

The award has served as a pretty telling litmus test for excellence since 14 winners have gone on to Hall of Fame careers. Rookies who played for the Dodgers have claimed the most awards from any franchise (16), with the New York Yankees ranking second (eight). Twice during the history of the award, the player named Rookie of the Year also claimed the league's MVP award, as Fred Lynn of the Red Sox and the Seattle Mariners' Ichiro Suzuki each turned the trick. Meanwhile, the Dodgers' Fernando Valenzuela is the only player to win the honor and the Cy Young Award in the same year.

Willie Mays became the first Giants player to win the award in 1951 when he hit .274 with 20 home runs and 68 RBIs. Seven years later, Orlando Cepeda became the second Giant to earn Rookie of the Year honors after hitting .312 with 25 home runs and 96 RBIs in 1958. The Giants cobbled together back-to-back winners in Cepeda and Willie McCovey, who claimed the award in 1959 when he hit .354 with 13 home runs and 38 RBIs.

Not until 1973, when outfielder Gary Matthews came up for the Giants, did the team have another winner. Matthews won the award after hitting .300 with 12 home runs and 58 RBIs. Two years later, John Montefusco became the first and only Giants rookie pitcher to win the award when he went 15–9 with a 2.88 ERA and 215 strikeouts in 34 starts in 1975. Buster Posey became the most recent Giants Rookie of the Year when he claimed the honor after the 2010 season.

Mays, Cepeda, and McCovey have all been enshrined in the Baseball Hall of Fame in Cooperstown, New York.

Dave Kingman

Dave Kingman's size drew attention whenever he stepped onto a baseball field. Standing 6'6", fans and opposing pitchers understood what such a body could do to a baseball if he made contact. Of course, that became a major problem for Kingman. While he could hit a home run during any given at-bat, each home run was balanced by approximately four strikeouts, which equated to a low batting average and on-base percentage. By the time he retired, he had accrued 442 home runs and 1,210 RBIs, but also amassed 1,816 Ks.

But when Kingman did make contact, there was nothing ordinary about his home runs, which earned him the nickname of "Kong" as he was the kind of player who prompted fans to delay trips to the concession stands until after he hit for fear they might miss something special.

Kingman had twice been drafted by the time the Giants used the first pick of the 1970 secondary-phase draft to select him. The California Angels had selected him in the second round of the 1967 draft, and the Baltimore Orioles selected him in the first round of the 1968 draft. Instead, he opted to play at the University of Southern California, where Trojans coach Rod Dedeaux changed him into a position player after he went to USC as a pitcher. Kingman slugged the Trojans to the College World Series, where they won the championship and he earned All-America honors along the way before the Giants brought him into the fold.

Giants fans eagerly awaited Kingman's arrival, and they finally got their wish on July 30, 1971, when he served as a pinch runner for future Hall of Fame first baseman Willie McCovey. He hit his first major league home run in the first game that followed and added two more the next day. While viewed only as a slugger, Kingman had multiple skills, which he demonstrated on April 16, 1972, when he hit for the cycle in a 10–6 Giants win. Kingman also showed flexibility in the field as he played third base, outfield, and first base. He even pitched two innings toward the end of a lopsided Giants loss to the Reds on April 15, 1973, and again almost a month later in a loss to the Dodgers.

While flexible, Kingman never seemed to master anything except the art of hitting a monster home run. Steve Ontiveros took Kingman's starting third-base job in 1974 after Kingman made 12 errors in 59 chances, leaving the slugger as a glorified pinch-hitter. The following season the Giants sold Kingman to the New York Mets. The Mets used Kingman primarily at first base and in the outfield, and he made progress in the field, which afforded him more opportunities to hit, and, thus, hit home runs. In his first season with the Mets, he clubbed 36 home runs and followed with 37 in 1976, including a memorable blast at Wrigley Field on April 14. Kingman hit a ball against the Cubs that day that many feel is the longest home run ever hit at the historic ballpark, estimated to have traveled 550 feet. Kong also hit three home runs in a game for the first time in 1976 when he turned the trick against the Dodgers in an 11–0 Mets win on June 4. He would go on to hit three home runs in a game five times in his career.

During his career, Kingman also would play with the San Diego Padres, California Angels, New York Yankees, Chicago Cubs, and the Oakland Athletics. His best season came in 1979 with the Cubs when he hit .288 with 48 home runs—which led the major leagues—and 115 RBIs. The well-traveled slugger retired after the 1986 season.

84 Herman Franks

Like many managers before him, Herman Franks did not show much as a player, but he did become a successful major league manager. A native of Price, Utah, Franks attended the University of Utah in advance of moving into the professional ranks in 1932 with the Hollywood Stars of the Pacific Coast League. A left-handed-hitting catcher, Franks showed enough promise to prompt the St. Louis Cardinals to purchase him from the Stars. Franks then seemed to vanish in the deep pool of players serving in the Cardinals' expansive farm system.

In 1939 Franks played in 17 games for the Cardinals, which served as a prelude for his exodus from St. Louis. The Brooklyn Dodgers acquired Franks prior to the 1940 season, and he became the team's backup catcher. Of utmost importance for Franks' future, being in the Dodgers organization allowed him to befriend Leo Durocher. Franks served as the team's backup through 1941 before he served in the military during World War II. Upon his return, he managed and played for the St. Paul Saints, the Dodgers' Triple A affiliate in the American Association. But he left the post in August 1947 to once again become a major league player, as he joined the Philadelphia Athletics, playing in 48 games during the 1947 and 1948 seasons.

After Durocher became manager of the Giants, Franks joined him as a coach in 1949, enjoying the ride while the Giants won the National League pennant in 1951 and 1954, in addition to the World Series title in 1954. During that stint, Franks was said to play an integral part in baseball history by stealing signs from the

Dodgers during the famed 1951 playoff game that culminated in Bobby Thomson's "Shot Heard Round the World" home run (see No. 88, "Read *The Echoing Green*").

Regardless of whether Franks actually stole signals on that historic day, he was a loyal Durocher follower, which instilled in him many of the same antics employed by Durocher. In other words, he adopted a win-at-all-costs attitude. At times this spilled over into classless actions such as going into the other team's clubhouse to drop the fact that the Giants' pitchers would be throwing at their heads that day, so don't dig in too firmly once in the batter's box. In Peter Golenbock's book, *Bums*, Carl Furillo is quoted about Durocher loyalists such as Franks, when he said, "They were dirty ballplayers.... They all wanted to be like Durocher, to copy Durocher. That Herman Franks, he was another one."

Franks left the Giants after the 1955 season, which coincided with Durocher's departure. He remained on the organization's payroll as a scout, a general manager for a minor league affiliate, and as a Giants coach before he took over as the team's manager prior to the 1965 season. Franks managed talented Giants teams that boasted of baseball heavyweights Juan Marichal, Gaylord Perry, Willie Mays, and Willie McCovey, but second place was the best they could do during his four seasons managing the team.

Franks' final season as the Giants manager came in 1968; Clyde King took over the following season. Franks left the game for a year but returned as a coach with the Chicago Cubs under Durocher in 1970 before again retiring. In 1977 he became manager of the Cubs and served in the role until resigning in September 1979. Franks hit just .199 as a player with three career home runs, but as a manager he was the equivalent of a .300 hitter, as he produced an impressive winning record of 605–521.

Felipe Alou

Felipe Alou holds the distinction of being the first Dominican Republic–born player to become a regular player in the major leagues. A native of Bajos de Haina, Dominican Republic, Alou's real last name is Rojas. However, he became "Alou" after the scout that signed him wrote the wrong name on the contract. Alou grew up poor and hoped to become a doctor. A talented track-and-field athlete, Alou went to the Pan-American games as a baseball player and proved to possess the special kind of talents that could better unlock the doors to a brighter future than chasing his dream of becoming a doctor.

Eventually, he agreed to join the Giants organization in 1955 by signing a contract that paid him a $200 bonus. By 1958 Alou had worked his way to the major leagues during the Giants' first season in San Francisco. In his fifth major league season in 1962, Alou became an All-Star during a season in which he hit .316 with 25 home runs and 98 RBIs. Though he had star qualities, Alou did not stand out on the Giants, a team that had many stars in Willie McCovey, Willie Mays, Juan Marichal, and Orlando Cepeda.

Though a force in the lineup, he soon became viewed simply as one of the Alou brothers after Felipe's younger brothers, Matty and Jesus, arrived in 1960 and '63, respectively, thereby setting the stage for a unique situation that saw the Giants use all of the Alou brothers in the outfield at the same time (see No. 23, "All Alou"). No further family reunions took place following the 1963 season, as the Giants traded Felipe to the Braves prior to the 1964 campaign. Alou hit .286 with 85 home runs and 325 RBIs in six seasons with the Giants.

Felipe Alou, one of three Alou brothers to play for the San Francisco Giants at the same time, slides into home plate during a game against the Milwaukee Braves in 1960. Alou would later manage the Giants from 2003 to 2006.

While with the Braves, he had his best season in 1966 when he hit .327 with 31 home runs and led the National League in hits (218), runs scored (122), and total bases (355). Ironically, he finished second in the National League batting race that year to his brother, Matty (.342). In 1968 Alou had another All-Star season when he hit .317, accruing 210 hits for the season. After playing with the Braves, Alou had stints with the Oakland A's, New York Yankees, Montreal Expos, and Milwaukee Brewers. He finished his 17-year major league career in 1974, having compiled a .286 lifetime batting average, 206 home runs, and 852 RBIs.

Alou became a batting instructor in the Montreal Expos organization in 1976, which led to his becoming a minor league manager. In 1985 the Giants needed a manager and looked to their former player, offering him the position. However, Alou did not take the job as he felt he owed it to the Expos to remain with their organization. The Expos rewarded Alou for his loyalty when they named him the team's manager on May 22, 1992, which made him the first Dominican-born manager in major league history.

Alou's arrival coincided with the arrival of a corps of young stars with the Expos. By 1994 the likes of Delino DeShields, Larry Walker, and Moises Alou, Felipe's son, were jelling and appeared to have the best team in baseball. Sadly for Alou and the Expos, the 1994 season turned out to be the year when a labor stoppage turned ugly and resulted in the cancellation of nearly two months of the season, as well as the postseason, thereby costing the Expos the best opportunity in the organization's history to win a world championship. After the strike-shortened season, the Expos began to gut the team. Despite the reduction of talent, Alou remained at the helm of the Expos and eventually became the team's most successful manager in its history.

Alou got fired during the 2001 season and did not manage again until the Giants finally brought him back to San Francisco prior to the 2003 season. He managed the Giants through the 2006 season, posting a 342–304 mark before leaving the team prior to the 2007 season.

86 Robb Nen

Robb Nen threw hard, threw strikes, and had a competitive nature. All were and still are necessary attributes to being a major league closer, and Nen thrived in the role. The son of Dick Nen, a former major league first baseman, Robb played baseball and football at

Los Alamitos High School in Los Alamitos, California. Nen could count among his teammates at Los Alamitos J.T. Snow, who would later become his teammate on the Giants.

Though Nen played third base in high school, pitching ultimately would be his calling, and he signed with the Texas Rangers after they drafted him to be a pitcher in the 32nd round of the 1987 draft. By 1993 Nen was in Arlington pitching in the major leagues. He got off to a disappointing start with the Rangers, posting a sky-high 6.35 ERA. Less than dazzled by the right-hander, the Rangers sent Nen and pitcher Kurt Miller to the Florida Marlins for pitcher Cris Carpenter. The Marlins identified Nen's strengths as a reliever and sent him to the bullpen in 1994, where he would take to the new role and find great success. He finished the strike-shortened 1994 season with 15 saves and a 2.95 ERA.

The right-hander had a unique delivery in which he strided toward the batter, allowing his lead foot to tap the mound mid-stride before fully extending and releasing the pitch. Nevertheless, Nen's fastball was clocked regularly in the upper 90-mph range. In addition to an explosive fastball, Nen possessed a devastating slider. He served as the Marlins' closer through the 1997 season, collecting 108 saves along the way to establish himself as one of the best closers in baseball. In 1997 he helped the Marlins win their first world championship, saving 35 games and posting a 9–3 record. Shortly after the Marlins defeated the Cleveland Indians in seven games in the World Series, the team was disbanded. The Giants traded Mike Pageler, Mike Villano, and Joe Fontenot to the Marlins to acquire Nen.

Nen took over the closer's role vacated by Rod Beck and Roberto Hernandez, who both left via free agency. Beck had accrued 199 saves in seven years as the Giants' closer, so he left big shoes to fill. Nen not only filled Beck's shoes, he outgrew them. In his first year with the Giants, he cashed in 40 saves with a 1.52 ERA and 110 strikeouts. He would go on to be selected to three All-Star

Games while with the Giants in 1998, 1999, and 2002. Giants fans were fond of Nen and appreciated his work as they began referring to the ninth inning as the "Nenth."

When the team moved from Candlestick Park to PacBell Park in 2000, Nen's entrance from the bullpen was accompanied by Deep Purple's "Smoke on the Water." In Nen's final four seasons with the Giants, he recorded 37, 41, 45, and 43 saves. Nen's final game in the major leagues came in Game 6 of the 2002 World Series. The Giants held a 5–0 lead before running into trouble in the seventh when Anaheim scored three. Angels center fielder Darin Erstad led off the bottom of the eighth with a home run to cut the Giants' lead to 5–4. After runners reached second and third with no outs, Nen came in to put out the fire and faced third baseman Troy Glaus. Unfortunately for Nen and the Giants, he surrendered a two-run double to Glaus that put the Angels ahead 6–5. They held on to win the game by that score and, after winning Game 7, took the World Series.

Nen spent two years trying to return from surgery that corrected a torn rotator cuff. When he filed for free agency and no teams attempted to pick him up prior to the 2005 season, Nen figured it was time to retire. In five seasons with the Giants, Nen accumulated 206 saves, giving him 314 for his career.

87 Bonds Joins 40-40 Club

Until Jose Canseco first hit 40 home runs and stole 40 bases in the same season, nobody had paid much attention to the feat. Upon further examination, the idea of any player having the diversified talents necessary to be able to enter the 40-40 club translated to a unique player. A player with extraordinary power, yet fast enough—and savvy enough—to steal bases against major league pitchers and catchers.

Such a breed was not the norm since most sluggers had no speed, while the jackrabbits didn't have the muscle, or the swing, to go deep. Canseco pulled off the feat in 1988 when he hit 42 home runs and stole 40 bases in 1988 for the Oakland Athletics. Prior to Canseco accomplishing the feat, several players had come close to reaching the mark.

Ken Williams of the St. Louis Browns hit 39 home runs and stole 37 bases in 1922. Though he became the first player to hit 30 home runs and steal 30 bases in the same season, he came up short of 40-40. But remember, the season lasted just 154 games in 1922. In 1957 Willie Mays stole 40 bases, but he came up four home runs short of becoming the first player to reach 40-40. Bobby Bonds had 38 home runs with 21 games remaining in the 1973 season, but Barry Bonds' father could not go yard until the season's final game and finished with 39 homers to go with his 43 stolen bases. Eric Davis and Darryl Strawberry came close in 1987 when Davis stole 50 and hit 37, while Strawberry stole 36 and hit 39.

Nevertheless, the idea of someone going 40-40 still wasn't widely thought of until Canseco began to chat up his chances. Suddenly, baseball fans began checking the daily box scores to see if he had hit a home run or stolen a base. Even Mickey Mantle weighed in by saying, "Hell, if I'd known 40-40 was going to be a big deal, I'd have done it every year!"

Bonds got the milestone in his mind and set out to reach the plateau his father had just barely missed. The question of whether he could pull it off came down to the final three games of the 1996 season. Bonds already had hit 42 home runs; all he lacked was a stolen base that would take him to 40 for the season. On September 27, 1996, more than 48,000 fans huddled in Coors Field to see the Giants play the Colorado Rockies. Many of them had turned out for the sole purpose of seeing if Bonds could match the record and share a piece of baseball history with Canseco. In Bonds' first at-bat, he drew a walk from Rockies starter Armando Reynoso, but the opportunity to steal a base did not present itself. Bonds batted again in the third inning with one out. After hitting a single, Glenallen Hill stepped to the plate, and that's when Bonds took off for second. When his foot hit the bag, second-base umpire Bob Davidson signaled safe, and Bonds had stolen his way into baseball history.

Only two other players have accomplished the feat since Bonds, as Alex Rodriguez did so with the Seattle Mariners in 1998 when he hit 42 and stole 46. Alfonso Soriano became the last major leaguer to go 40-40 when he stole 41 and hit 46 in 2006 for the Washington Nationals.

88 Read *The Echoing Green*

Say it ain't so…

According to author Joshua Prager's 2006 book, *The Echoing Green: The Untold Story of Bobby Thomson, Ralph Branca, and the Shot Heard Round the World*, the most famous home run in major league history might not have happened had the Giants not been stealing signals during the third game of the 1951 playoff between the Brooklyn Dodgers and the Giants.

A writer at the *Wall Street Journal*, Prager wrote a narrative that gives another look at what happened during that memorable game, lending a sense of espionage to the events leading up to Thomson's fateful swing. Prager's account alleges that Giants coach and manager Leo Durocher's protégé, Herman Franks, positioned himself inside the home clubhouse at Polo Grounds, which sat in center field. From that post, Franks was said to have viewed

Dodgers catcher Rube Walker's signals to the pitcher by looking through a telescope. Once Franks knew what the pitch would be, he quickly sent the information to the Giants' backup catcher, Sal Yvars, who then signaled the hitters from the bullpen.

Prager actually broke the story in 2001, and part of the book covers the aftermath of the story as it related to Branca, who surrendered the home run, and Thomson. After surrendering the home run, Branca became the punchline for fatal outcomes, while Thomson became a celebrated hero. Branca became aware of what happened through Yvars, which generated a great deal of angst in Branca and left him with hard feelings toward Thomson, who never admitted to taking advantage of the information. In the end, the pair reconciled, which led to their to becoming friends as well as business partners who profited from the historic event.

Prager offers an insightful look at New York City baseball during the era and gives perspective into the lives of the participants in the Giants' shenanigans, such as Hank Schenz, the utility infielder who owned the 35mm Wollensak telescope that Franks looked through to heist the signs. And there is Abe Chadwick, an electrician who worked at the Polo Grounds and rigged the buzzer that was used to send the signals from Franks to Yvars in the bullpen. Ironically, Chadwick was a rabid Dodgers fan and had no idea of his part in the episode. Finally, the book takes a look at Franks, who comes off as a brilliant baseball man for his ability to quickly decipher the signals before relaying them to the bullpen. He is also depicted almost as a blind disciple of Durocher, who would literally do anything to win a baseball game. Franks once was asked where he had been when Thomson hit his home run, and he answered, "Doing something for Durocher."

Thomson's blast happened during the "golden age" of baseball, back when the game reigned as the country's most popular sport, and New York served as its mecca. Did Thomson know the pitch before he hit the home run? Despite evidence suggesting he did, we'll never really know because Thomson died in 2010. And besides, if you're a Giants fan, you don't really care because, to paraphrase famed Giants radio broadcaster Russ Hodges after Thomson's home run, "The Giants won the pennant! The Giants won the pennant!"

Regardless, Prager's book is a must-read for any Giants fan.

89 Kong's Bomb Wins the Division

On September 30, 1971, the Giants found themselves in a place they never thought they would be on the final day of the season: fighting to earn a spot in the postseason. On September 4, the Giants held an 8½-game lead over the second-place Dodgers. By September 16, the Dodgers had cut the lead to one game, giving the Giants' archrivals the look of a team destined to steal away the National League West title that seemed to be the Giants' from the start of the season.

Willie McCovey, Juan Marichal, and Willie Mays were all past their prime, but each of them remained a quality major league player. As a group, this future Hall of Fame trio had played in just one World Series as the San Francisco Giants, and that had been nine years earlier when they won the National League pennant before losing to the Yankees in the World Series.

The Giants had lost 16 of 26 games in September and felt like they were in a free fall. Yet they went to the final day of the season holding their destiny in their own hands. If the Giants wanted to return to the postseason, they needed to find success against the San Diego Padres in their final game. If they did not win, and the Dodgers defeated the Houston Astros that day, the Giants and Dodgers would tie for the West title.

Needing a quality pitching effort, Giants manager Charlie Fox handed the ball to Marichal. Though the game was played in San Diego, a large contingent of Giants fans could be counted among the crowd of 34,861 in San Diego Stadium. Unfortunately for the Giants, they were without one of their best players that day. Bobby Bonds was injured and unable to play, leaving the outfield duty to Dave Kingman, aka "Kong"—the moniker given Kingman for his epic home runs. The rookie played right field and batted fifth in the lineup against left-hander Dave Roberts.

Three scoreless innings passed while the scoreboard flashed the news from Los Angeles, where the Dodgers had defeated the Astros 2–1. Tito Fuentes led off the fourth with a single to left. Mays followed with an RBI double to left to give the Giants a 1–0 lead. All month long, the Giants had struggled and seemingly experienced every possible negative outcome no matter what the situation suggested might happen. So a 1–0 lead did not feel safe. The Giants knew that they needed to build on that lead to give Marichal a cushion to work with, and they needed to get as much as they could against Roberts when the opportunity to do so presented itself. Roberts wasn't about to give in, and he retired McCovey on a lineout to center field to bring Kingman to the plate with one out and Mays still at second.

Kingman, who would hit 442 home runs in his career, faced a 1–1 count when Roberts delivered his third pitch. The 6'6" Kingman swung and connected, sending a drive into the left-field stands to give the Giants a 3–0 lead. Suddenly the Giants were in control.

Using his extensive repertoire of pitches, Marichal went the distance, holding the Padres to one run on five hits and no walks to earn his fourth consecutive win as the Giants took a 5–1 win to earn a place in the 1971 postseason.

Mike McCormick

Mike McCormick became the first Giants player to win a Cy Young Award and also owned the distinction of being the first member of the San Francisco Giants to throw a no-hitter—until that distinction was taken away.

Virtually every team in the major leagues had their eyes on the left-hander from Alhambra, California. At the age of 17, McCormick had been dazzling. He threw four no-hitters for his American Legion team, struck out 26 batters in one game, and went 49–4. While his record certainly was impressive, the manner in which he achieved the record brought more rave reviews. He had a flawless delivery and a big fastball.

Eventually, the New York Giants won the bidding war for McCormick that saw them pay him a $60,000 bonus—in 1956 dollars. Under the prevailing rules in baseball at the time, McCormick had to go straight to the major leagues, which resulted in some difficult outings. He made two starts and appeared in three games in 1956 and came away with an 0–1 record with a 9.45 ERA. The following season at the age of 18, he settled down some, making 24 appearances—five of them starts—before finishing at 3–1 with a 4.10 ERA. McCormick returned to the starting rotation in 1958, the Giants' first season in San Francisco, going 11–8 with a 4.59 ERA in 42 appearances, of which 28 were starts.

On June 12, 1959, he became the first Giants pitcher to throw a no-hitter in San Francisco when he no-hit the Philadelphia Phillies. Several interesting tidbits evolved from that outing. Back in 1959 a major league pitcher was credited for throwing a no-hitter even if it did not go the complete nine innings. McCormick's no-no had been of the five-inning variety. Until 1991 that no-hitter continued to be recognized as an official no-hitter. But that classification changed once the major leagues ruled that a pitcher must have thrown a complete game, nine-inning no-hitter to qualify for said distinction. Ironically, McCormick's no-hitter initially had become a no-hitter after he had allowed a hit. He had pitched five complete innings at Philadelphia, then gave up a hit in the sixth inning, but rain halted the game, so the game went back to the fifth inning and was considered an official game.

McCormick continued to mature on the mound. In 1960, at the age of 21, he posted a 15–12 record with a 2.70 ERA, which was the top ERA in the National League. McCormick experienced some arm problems, and his results suffered. He went 18–21 from 1961 to 1962, and the Giants traded him to the Baltimore Orioles. He continued to struggle with the Orioles and went to the minor leagues, returning to the major leagues with the Washington Senators.

In December 1966 the Giants brought him back to San Francisco in a trade. Though McCormick no longer had the big fastball, he had developed into a pitcher along the way, which included his adding a screwball to his repertoire. Relying on the screwball and his pitching education, McCormick's return to the Giants in 1967 was nothing short of sensational as he went 22–10 with a 2.85 ERA; he also pitched 14 complete games along with five shutouts. In doing so, he won the National League's Comeback Player of the Year award as well as the NL Cy Young Award, making him the first member of the Giants to win the coveted pitching award.

Tim Lincecum, who has won the Cy Young Award twice, in 2008 and 2009, is the only other Giants pitcher to win the award.

91 The Count

San Francisco fans fell in love with John Montefusco from the beginning, and "the Count" rewarded the Giants' faithful with many memorable moments. Montefusco hailed from Long Branch, New Jersey, where he fell in love with the game of baseball, but the game wasn't particularly enamored with him as a youngster. Montefusco was slight of build and did not even start pitching until his senior year of high school. Despite going 6–0 with a no-hitter, he went undrafted after graduation. So he headed to Brookdale Community College in Lincroft, New Jersey. After having great success at Brookdale, he still was overlooked. So he entered the working force and played semipro baseball.

Somehow, Montefusco caught the Giants' attention, and they signed the right-hander as an amateur free agent in 1972. By 1974 he made his major league debut at the age of 24. On September 3, 1974, Ron Bryant started for the Giants against the Dodgers and got into a first-inning mess when he allowed four runs—three earned—on a hit and four walks, without retiring a batter. Giants manager Wes Westrum had told Montefusco he would be the first guy out of the bullpen to enter the game, but Montefusco never expected to be entering the game in the first inning. Westrum had seen enough, so Montefusco entered the game with the bases loaded. Not only did Montefusco escape the first by retiring the three batters he faced—two by strikeout—he also pitched nine innings, allowing just one run to spur a 9–5 Giants win while earning his first major league win.

Making the day even more special for Montefusco was the fact that he homered off Charlie Hough in his first major league at-bat

John Montefusco prepares to deliver the ball to home plate during a game at Candlestick Park in 1976. He made the All-Star team that year, going 16–14 with a 2.84 ERA, and also pitched a no-hitter against the Atlanta Braves.

in the top of the third. Montefusco topped off his debut by saying all the right things afterward, specifically when asked about the Dodgers as he said, "I wanted to beat the Dodgers—I hate the Dodgers, I'm from New Jersey, and I've always been a Yankee fan."

He went on to post a 3–2 record with a 4.81 ERA in seven appearances—five of which were starts—for the Giants in 1974. Giants pitching coach Don McMahon would say about Montefusco, "Electricity just seems to purr from him. It's in his smile, his refreshing honesty, and his arm."

The following season, Montefusco found himself in the starting rotation and dazzled National League hitters en route to a 15–9 rookie season that featured a 2.88 ERA in 35 games. He pitched 10 complete games and four shutouts along the way, earning National League Rookie of the Year honors. He enjoyed great popularity with the Giants, earning the catchy nickname of "the Count," which was based on his last name sounding like "Monte Cristo." San Francisco's then-announcer Al Michaels is credited for coming up with "the Count of Montefusco," which evolved into simply "the Count."

In 1976 Montefusco made the National League All-Star team and finished the season at 16–14 with a 2.84 ERA. That season also would see Montefusco throw a no-hitter against the Atlanta Braves on September 29, 1976, in a 9–0 Giants win.

Montefusco fought injuries and mediocrity, which resulted in his being traded to the Braves in 1981 for Doyle Alexander. Montefusco went 59–62 in seven seasons for the Giants with a 3.47 ERA. After pitching one season for the Braves, he finished his major league career pitching for the San Diego Padres and New York Yankees. In 13 major league seasons, he went 90–83 with a 3.54 ERA. The Count remains one of the all-time crowd favorites in the history of Giants baseball in San Francisco.

Brian Sabean

Obviously, what happens on the field is the most important thing in a baseball game. But what happens off the field often dictates what happens on the field, which is why any team that wants to be good needs to have a quality general manager calling the shots. In Brian Sabean, the Giants have had one of the best in the business for many years and perhaps the best GM in the organization's modern history.

On September 30, 1996, Sabean became the Giants' senior vice president and general manager. Since taking over the position, Sabean's Giants teams have won a World Series in 2010, two

National League pennants (2002 and 2010), four NL West Division flags (1997, 2000, 2003, and 2010), a wild-card spot (2002), and forced a wild-card playoff game with the Chicago Cubs at the end of the 1998 season. By claiming the five playoff berths during Sabean's tenure, the Giants have accrued more than half of the organization's postseason appearances since the team moved to San Francisco in 1958.

Sabean graduated from Concord High School in Concord, New Hampshire, in 1974. After graduating from Eckerd College in St. Petersburg, Florida, in 1978, he served as an assistant baseball coach at St. Leo College in 1979 and the University of Tampa from 1980 to 1982. In 1983 Sabean was promoted to head coach at Tampa, where he held the position for two years, making the school's first appearance in an NCAA regional tournament in 1984 while putting together a 61–36 record.

Sabean worked eight years in the New York Yankees organization, holding several different positions before progressing to the organization's director of scouting from 1986 to 1990 and vice president of player development/scouting from 1990 to 1992. While with the Yankees, they drafted or signed Derek Jeter, Mariano Rivera, J.T. Snow, Jorge Posada, and Andy Pettitte.

Once he moved to the Giants, he served three years as the assistant to the general manager and vice president of scouting/player personnel before moving up to the position of senior vice president of player personnel in 1995. After becoming the general manager, Sabean has been proactive in making trades, signing free agents, and cultivating young talent. One of Sabean's most controversial trades came on November 13, 1996, when he sent Matt Williams and Trent Hubbard to the Cleveland Indians for Jeff Kent, Julian Tavarez, Jose Vizcaino, and Joe Roa. Williams had been popular with the fans, in addition to being one of the team's best sluggers in recent memory. In the aftermath of the deal, Sabean often found himself having to defend his moves. But history would prove how savvy Sabean had been in pulling the trigger. In six seasons with the Giants, Kent hit .297 with 175 home runs and 689 RBIs and won the National League MVP award in 2000.

Other notable moves on Sabean's résumé are the acquisitions of Jason Schmidt, Robb Nen, Kenny Lofton, Andres Galarraga, Ellis Burks, Joe Carter, Roberto Hernandez, Wilson Alvarez, and Jose Mesa.

In deference to other GMs and organizations, Sabean has not been enamored with counting on the June draft to build his team. He told the *San Francisco Chronicle*, "Quite frankly, we're very reluctant to overspend in the draft. We're cautious in that regard because it's so fallible. Our focus is spending as much as we can and being as wise as we can at the major league level and using the minor leagues as a supplement and not necessarily leaning on it totally. Teams that are allowed to have a three- to five-year plan and allowed to lose or explain to their fans they're in a rebuilding mode have a greater latitude than we do. We always have to be in a reloading mode."

Sabean was recognized as the Major League Baseball Executive of the Year by the *Sporting News* and *Baseball America* in 2003.

Buck Ewing

In the pioneer days of what comprised the major leagues prior to the 20th century, the Giants were known as the New York Gothams. Buck Ewing played catcher for the Gothams and generally was regarded not only as the best catcher, but also the best player in the game.

Ewing joined the Troy Trojans of the National League in September of 1880 at the age of 20. He played with the Trojans through 1882 before signing with the Giants as a free agent prior to the 1883 season. Once in New York, Ewing thrived.

Home runs had not entered the major league scene at that point and were more of an oddity than a reality. But that did not stop the 5′10″, 190-pound native of Hoagland, Ohio, from hitting round-trippers in his first season with the Giants. During that inaugural season in New York, Ewing became the first player in National League history to end the season with double-digit home runs, as he hit 10 in 88 games.

Triples were more common during Ewing's era due to the spacious ballparks and the fact that balls were not as well constructed as the modern ball would be. In addition to being able to hit a home run, Ewing could make a nice accounting for himself where triples were concerned, as he led the league in 1884 with 20 triples.

If there was a Johnny Bench before the 20th century, Ewing would have been the guy. Behind the plate he had no peers. Ewing loved to throw out opposing base runners, but opposing players were reluctant to afford him the opportunity, so Ewing would bait them into trying to advance. On numerous occasions, he purposely let the ball get away from him to entice the runner to take a chance. Once his prey took the bait by trying to advance, Ewing would unleash his cannon of an arm and make a perfect throw to nail the runner.

Such methodology did not surprise those who played with Ewing, as he was one of the smartest players in the game and was always thinking about baseball. He also is credited for being the first to hold a pregame clubhouse meeting. Ewing had such incredible instincts and talents behind the plate that John Foster, the editor of the *Spalding Guide*, wrote the following about Ewing in the 1938 edition: "As a thrower to bases, Ewing never had a superior, and there are not to exceed 10 men who could come anywhere near being equal to him. Ewing was the man of whom it was said, 'He handed the ball to the second baseman from the batter's box.'"

Roger Bresnahan

Initially, Roger Bresnahan pitched in the major leagues and actually threw a six-hit, complete game shutout on August 27, 1897. However, Bresnahan's value as a catcher had not yet been discovered at that point. Once his catching skills became apparent, he would remain behind the plate. Giants manager John McGraw called Bresnahan one of the best who ever played the position, which was high praise for the native of Ohio, given the lack of compliments issued by the tough taskmaster McGraw.

Bresnahan began his career with the Washington Senators in 1897 before going to the Chicago Orphans/Cubs in 1900 and the Baltimore Orioles from 1901 to 1902. Then the New York Giants grabbed him. He would play for the Giants from 1902 to 1908. In those seven seasons, Bresnahan hit .293 with 15 home runs and 291 RBIs. While with the Giants, Bresnahan and Hall of Fame hurler Christy Mathewson grew to have a great chemistry as battery mates.

In 1907 while still wearing the orange and black, Bresnahan became the first major league catcher to adopt the use of shin guards. Thus many future backstops had Bresnahan to thank for saving them from the bumps, bruises, and broken legs that otherwise would have befallen them. Bresnahan finished his career with stints playing for the St. Louis Cardinals and Cubs. He retired after the 1915 season. He also served as a player/manager for both the Cardinals and Cubs. He was elected to the Baseball Hall of Fame in 1945.

While Ewing ranked as the top catcher in the game, he also had great versatility due to his athleticism. During his career, he played every position in the field at one time or another. His athleticism also translated to his speed, which fueled 354 stolen bases during his 18 seasons in the major leagues.

The Giants traded Ewing to the Cleveland Spiders for George Davis in 1893. In nine seasons with the Giants, Ewing hit .306 with 47 home runs, 459 RBIs, and 109 triples. Ewing's first season with the Spiders proved to be his best in the major leagues when he hit .344 with six home runs, 122 RBIs, and 47 stolen bases. He played two seasons for Cleveland before playing the final three seasons of his major league career with the Cincinnati Reds. He retired after the 1897 season. Ewing was elected to the Baseball Hall of Fame by the Old-Timers Committee in 1939.

94 400-400 Club

Bobby Bonds came up 68 home runs short of becoming the first player in major league history to hit 400 home runs and steal 400 bases. However, the apple didn't fall too far from the tree when the first player to turn the trick turned out to be Bonds' son, Barry. Bobby Bonds had been a Giants All-Star (see No. 19, "Bobby Bonds") of extraordinary athletic skills during his playing career. He passed on the same athletic skills that fueled his career to his son, Barry, and the heir took those skills to another level.

Barry Bonds had been an above-average base stealer early in his career, stealing 30-plus bases for nine seasons. He reached a career high in 1990 when he stole 52 while still playing for the Pirates. A player's legs normally slow down before the speed of a player's bat, which is what happened with Bonds, who entered the Giants' July 26, 1997, game against the Pittsburgh Pirates with 399 stolen bases.

Candlestick Park hosted a crowd of 25,962 that day, and they hoped to see Bonds reach base and get the opportunity to steal. Esteban Loaiza started for the Pirates and struck out Bonds looking in the first inning. In the fourth inning, Loaiza again had his way with the Giants slugger, who watched strike three pass by him for a second time.

Brian Johnson homered to start the Giants' fifth. Then pitcher Doug Creek singled, followed by a ground-rule double by Darryl Hamilton. A ground-out scored Creek and moved Hamilton to third, bringing Bonds to the plate for his third at-bat. Loaiza opted to intentionally walk Bonds. Jeff Kent followed with a single to score Hamilton and advance Bonds to second with one out. With J.T. Snow at the plate, Bonds and Kent executed a double steal to put both runners in scoring position and give Bonds his 400th career stolen base, putting him halfway to the 400-400 milestone; he lacked only a 400th home run.

Bonds and the Giants played the Florida Marlins in Miami on August 23, 1998. Bonds entered the game with 399 career home runs, leaving him one home run short of becoming baseball's first 400-home-run, 400-stolen-base player. Facing Marlins left-hander Kirt Ojala in the first inning, Bonds just got underneath a pitch and flew out to left field.

He would not miss in his next at-bat. A crowd of 36,701 watched at Pro Player Stadium, hoping to see baseball history. In the second inning, Bill Mueller hit the Giants' first home run off Ojala with Ellis Burks and Charlie Hayes aboard to give the Giants a 3–0 lead. Rich Aurilia grounded out to start the Giants third and bring Bonds to the plate to again face Ojala. After the count moved to 1–1, Bonds picked out a pitch he liked and ripped the ball down the right-field line that ducked into the stands just fair for a home run. Bonds rounded the bases, and when his foot touched down on home plate, he had become the first player in baseball history to have 400 home runs and 400 stolen bases.

To put Bonds' accomplishment into perspective, the only other players in baseball history who've come close to the 400-400 club are Willie Mays and Andre Dawson, both of whom have more than 400 homers and 300 steals.

95 Greg Minton

Greg Minton turned a severe injury into an advantage and went on to become one of the best relievers in Giants history. A native Texan, Minton grew up in San Diego, where he enjoyed surfing and didn't really concentrate on baseball until after his father told him he wasn't going to foot the bill for college tuition. He ended up playing shortstop for his high school team and earned a scholarship to San Diego Mesa Junior College, where his strong arm caught the attention of the Kansas City Royals. They ended up drafting Minton in the third round of the 1970 June draft and converted him into a pitcher. After Minton spent three seasons in the Royals organization, they traded him to the Giants on April 2, 1973, for catcher Fran Healy.

Two years later, Minton arrived to the major leagues with the Giants in 1975. He would spend parts of the next four seasons with the Giants, shuffling back and forth between the major leagues and Giants farm teams. During his tenure in the minor leagues, Minton became a living legend for his penchant for mischief. Among his antics were flooding a minor league ballpark to have a game canceled—and remember, this was before the movie *Bull Durham*. He once hijacked the team bus and was forever stealing the keys to the bullpen cart that took relievers into the game. Later he got the nickname "Moon Man" after getting sunburned while tubing down a river naked.

Minton's fastball registered in the 92–93 mph range on a regular basis, but the ball had little movement, which explained why major league, as well as minor league, hitters knocked him around. Then he tore the cartilage in his knee in spring training in 1978, and what could have been a devastating injury turned into a career-changing event.

Upon returning to the Giants, he pitched batting practice, and lo and behold, he suddenly had movement on his pitches. Out of necessity due to the limitations of his knee, he had to adjust his leg kick, and his ball began to sink. A changed man with the Giants in 1979, Minton pitched in 46 games, went 4–3 with a 1.81 ERA and collected four saves without allowing a home run. The next season he took over the Giants' closer role for good. In 1980 he went 4–6 with a 2.46 ERA and 19 saves, followed by seasons of 21, 30, 22, and 19 saves. In 1980, and again in 1981, he did not give up a single round-tripper. In fact, between the homer he allowed to Joe Ferguson of the Dodgers on September 6, 1978, and the home run the Mets' John Stearns hit off him on May 2, 1982, Minton went an astonishing 270⅓ innings without allowing a home run. Minton held the major league record for games pitched in a season without allowing a home run until George Sherrill broke his mark in 2006.

Minton's best season with the Giants came in 1982 when he made the All-Star team and finished the season at 10-4 with a 1.83 ERA and 30 saves. Gradually, his numbers began to decline until he lost his closing duties to Scott Garrelts in 1985. After a slow start in 1987, the Giants released Minton. In 13 seasons with the Giants, he went 45–52 with a 3.23 ERA and 125 saves. Minton experienced a modest comeback with the California Angels when he went 5–4 with 10 saves and a 3.08 ERA in 1987. He pitched four seasons with the Angels before retiring after the 1990 season at the age of 38. He is remembered as one of the great characters in Giants history, as well as a fine reliever.

96 Rich Aurilia

During Rich Aurilia's 15-year major league career, most of which was spent with the Giants, he brought his teams a rare breed of shortstop: one who could hit with power. Aurilia hailed from Brooklyn, New York, and played collegiately at St. John's University. He became an All–Big East selection in 1992 in advance of the Texas Rangers drafting him in the 24th round of the 1992 major league draft.

After three seasons in the Rangers' farm system, Aurilia went to the Giants along with Desi Wilson in a trade that sent John Burkett to the Rangers on December 22, 1994. Aurilia got his first taste of the major leagues when he made his debut on September 6, 1995, at the age of 24 and hit .474 in nine games, which included two home runs and four RBIs. He did not earn a regular spot in the lineup until 1998, when he played in 122 games and hit .266 with nine home runs and 49 RBIs. His breakthrough season came the following year when he hit .281 with 22 home runs and 80 RBIs.

Aurilia hit 79 home runs from 1999 through 2001, which led all National League shortstops. Included in that solid run was his best season, which took place in 2001. Aurilia hit .324—fueled by a National League–leading 206 hits—with 37 home runs and 97 RBIs. Aurilia made his one and only All-Star team in 2001. In addition, he won a Silver Slugger award, given to the best hitter at each position in each league. Aurilia's season was overshadowed by Barry Bonds, who set the single-season home run record by hitting 73 home runs. Of course, having Aurilia in the lineup helped Bonds see more good pitches than he might otherwise have seen.

Aurilia's offensive production began to slow down following 2001, when he dropped to .257 with 15 home runs and 61 RBIs in 2002. However, he did manage to contribute greatly to the Giants' offense during their World Series run, when they lost in seven games to the Angels. In 17 postseason games, Aurilia hit .265 with six home runs and 17 RBIs.

Aurilia's power numbers continued to tumble in 2003 when he hit .277 with 13 home runs and 58 RBIs. After nine seasons with the Giants, Aurilia signed with the Seattle Mariners as a free agent prior to the 2004 season. After playing in just 73 games for the Mariners, Aurilia was traded to the San Diego Padres. Aurilia struggled at the plate at both stops, and the Padres did not tender him a contract for the 2005 season. He ended up signing to play for the Reds in 2005 and rebounded nicely with a .282 average, 14 home runs, and 68 RBIs. He played another season for the Reds in 2006, rotating between all the infield positions, and had another good offensive season by hitting .300 with 23 home runs and 70 RBIs.

He returned to the Giants in 2007 and spent the final three seasons of his career in San Francisco. Aurilia's final home game came on October 1, when the Giants hosted the Arizona Diamondbacks at AT&T Park. In a nice gesture by Giants fans, Aurilia received a standing ovation. In 12 seasons with the Giants, Aurilia hit .275 with 143 home runs and 574 RBIs. Overall, Aurilia hit .275 with 186 RBIs and 756 RBIs in 15 major league seasons.

97 1961 All-Star Game

In what proved to be a salute to San Francisco, Major League Baseball awarded the 1961 midsummer classic—or one of that summer's two midsummer classics—to San Francisco. Beginning in 1959 Major League Baseball held two All-Star Games, with the idea being that more fans could be exposed to the game this way. The practice of holding two All-Star Games only lasted through the 1962 season.

The 1961 All-Star Games were played in San Francisco and Boston on July 11 and July 31, respectively. Candlestick Park, which was being heralded as a modern marvel due to the fact it was the major leagues' first all-concrete stadium, was hosting the game in just its second year of operation, and the game would prove memorable.

The Stick swelled with a capacity crowd of 44,115. Four Giants were on the National League team—Willie Mays, Mike McCormick, Orlando Cepeda, and Stu Miller—and the game itself would feature 18 future Hall of Fame players on the American and National League rosters. Among those future Hall of Famers were the starting pitchers: Whitey Ford of the New York Yankees and

Warren Spahn of the Milwaukee Braves. The National League held a 2–0 lead after five innings when Harmon Killebrew of the Minnesota Twins hit a solo home run in the sixth off McCormick to cut the lead in half.

George Altman of the Chicago Cubs hit a solo home run off Mike Fornieles of the Boston Red Sox in the eighth to give the National League a 3–1 lead heading into the final inning, which is when the game got really interesting. The American League cut the lead to 3–2 and had runners on first and second with Miller, the Giants right-hander, on the mound. At that juncture of the game, the winds at Candlestick Park picked up, which facilitated one of the odder sights ever seen in a baseball game. Miller had just gone into his set position on the mound when a gust of wind blew, and Miller moved just enough to result in a balk being called, moving the runners to second and third. The tying run then crossed the plate on an error by third baseman Ken Boyer.

The game went into extra innings, and the American League pushed across a run in the top of the 10th to take a 4–3 lead. Knuckleball specialist Hoyt Wilhelm of the Baltimore Orioles started the bottom of the 10th for the American League, hoping to get the necessary three outs to earn the junior circuit a victory. But the National League put together a rally in their half of the inning that had a distinct Hall of Fame flavor. Hank Aaron of the Braves singled to start the National League rally. Mays then drove home Aaron with a double. After Frank Robinson was hit by a pitch, Pittsburgh Pirates great Roberto Clemente hit a game-winning single. A jubilant Mays crossed home plate with the winning run, affording the hometown fans the thrill of seeing the Giants' biggest hero give the National League a 5–4 win.

The second All-Star Game of 1961 took place at Boston's Fenway Park. That game also would bring an oddity. That game was tied 1–1 after nine innings when it began to rain and did not stop, which resulted in the first tie game in All-Star Game history.

98 2007 All-Star Game

AT&T Park hosted the 78th All-Star Game, and the festivities proved to be a celebration of San Francisco as well as a good game to watch. While the city of San Francisco was in the spotlight, Ichiro Suzuki of the Seattle Mariners stole the show.

The National League led the game 1–0 in the top of the fifth when Brian Roberts reached with a leadoff walk. One out later, Ichiro stepped to the plate. The Mariners outfielder was the picture of confidence, having already singled in his first two at-bats. Chris Young of the San Diego Padres delivered, and Ichiro swung at the first pitch, sending a drive down the right-field line. Cincinnati Reds outfielder Ken Griffey Jr. raced toward the line to field the drive, but rather than making the expected rebound, the ball ricocheted in another direction. The fleet-footed Ichiro scooted around the bases with Roberts touching home just ahead of him to give the American League a 2–1 lead and Ichiro the first inside-the-park home run in All-Star Game history. "I thought it was going to go over the fence," said Ichiro afterward. "When it didn't, I was really bummed."

After the inning concluded, Griffey reported that he asked Giants left fielder Barry Bonds if he'd seen such a play take place at AT&T Park. "Barry said he's never seen that happen," said Griffey, who drove in two runs via a first-inning single and a sixth-inning sacrifice fly.

The American League added more conventional home runs to the party as Carl Crawford of the Tampa Bay Devil Rays hit one off the Milwaukee Brewers' Francisco Cordero in the sixth—on a ball that appeared to be interfered with by a fan, though fan interference was not called—and Victor Martinez of the Cleveland Indians followed suit in the eighth off the Mets' Billy Wagner.

The National League trailed 5–2 heading into the ninth, but still managed to make a game of it. With two outs in the ninth, the senior circuit came to life. Washington's Dmitri Young singled before Alfonso Soriano of the Cubs homered off Seattle's J.J. Putz. Three walks followed to load the bases; two of the walks were issued by the Angels' closer, Francisco Rodriguez, who took over for Putz. K-Rod finished off the game by getting Aaron Rowand of the Philadelphia Phillies to fly out to right field to end the game.

Some questioned National League manager Tony LaRussa's decision to not pinch-hit the Cardinals' Albert Pujols for Rowand. LaRussa, the St. Louis manager, said he needed to keep Pujols available in case the game moved to extra innings. By winning, the American League extended its unbeaten streak to 11 games, which included the tie that took place in the 2002 game. In addition, the American League gained home-field advantage for the World Series with the victory.

A festive crowd of 43,965 had packed the stands at AT&T Park, and they made it clear throughout the evening that their rooting interests remained with the Giants. Bonds received a huge ovation, as did Hall of Fame outfielder Willie Mays, when the Giants icon was honored during a pregame ceremony.

Giants fans also showed that they don't forget. When Rodriguez and John Lackey were introduced prior to the game, they were showered with good-natured boos, as the pair had helped lead the Angels over the Giants in the 2002 World Series. And, of course, they saved some of their booing for the National Leaguers, too. When members of the Dodgers were introduced, the boos were more heartfelt. Ichiro won the game's Most Valuable Player award, but clearly, AT&T Park was the biggest star of the 2007 midsummer classic.

99 Randy Johnson Gets 300th Win

The body of Randy Johnson's work in the major leagues had been composed by the time he joined the Giants in 2009, but the 6'9" left-hander known as "the Big Unit" saved one last memorable snapshot for the Orange and Black faithful.

Johnson came to the Giants on December 26, 2008, needing just five wins to reach 300, the magic number for pitchers aiming for baseball immortality and a place in Cooperstown. Johnson began his career with the Montreal Expos. Back then, his every start brought an exercise in mechanics. Standing as tall as he did, he had a lot of moving parts, which resulted in prolonged bouts with control issues. However, once Johnson got his control, he soared. But the Expos were not the beneficiaries of Johnson's discovered mechanics, rather the Mariners were, as Johnson went to Seattle in a May 25, 1989, trade.

In 10 seasons with the Mariners, the Big Unit went 130–74 with a 3.42 ERA in 274 games before he was sent to the Houston Astros, who were trying to win a pennant in 1998. After his brief stop in Houston, Johnson went to the Arizona Diamondbacks as a free agent prior to the 1999 season and became an integral part of the D'backs capturing the 2001 National League pennant and winning the World Series. In eight seasons in Arizona, Johnson went 118–62 with a 2.83 ERA. He then went to the New York Yankees for two seasons before returning to Arizona for two seasons prior to joining the Giants.

On June 4, Johnson took the mound against the Washington Nationals in his first opportunity to capture his 300th win. Johnson seemed to reverse time while holding the Nationals hitless through four innings, leaving the crowd at Nationals Park hanging on the edge of their seats while wondering if they would get to see Johnson throw a no-no on the same night he reached the hallowed pitching milestone.

After allowing one earned run on two hits through six innings, Johnson hit the turf while fielding a ball before making the throw to first base for the first out of the seventh. He bruised his shoulder on the play and had to leave the game after throwing just 78 pitches with the Giants leading 2–1. Johnson had done his part and retreated to the clubhouse to watch the game on TV, waiting to see if he would in fact become the sixth left-hander in major league history to accrue 300 wins.

First he watched the seventh and eighth innings get successfully navigated without a run scoring as Giants relievers Brandon Medders, Jeremy Affeldt, and Brian Wilson all did their jobs—but not without a little controversy. With the bases loaded and two out, Adam Dunn faced a 3–2 pitch from Wilson. The fastball looked low, which would have been ball four and forced home the tying run, thereby giving Johnson a no-decision. Instead, home-plate umpire Tim Timmons called the pitch strike three, much to Dunn's chagrin.

Johnson then returned to the dugout to see if the lead would stand. The Giants padded their lead with three runs in the ninth thanks largely to Randy Winn's two-run double, and Wilson successfully preserved the win in the bottom half of the inning to allow history to happen. By reaching the milestone, Johnson earned the distinction of becoming the first pitcher since Tom Seaver in 1985 to claim his 300th win in his first attempt. At the age of 45 years, 267 days, Johnson also became the second-oldest pitcher to win 300 games; Phil Niekro was the oldest at the age of 46, 188 days. Despite having reached a milestone that only 23 others in baseball history had accomplished, Johnson kept his accomplishment in perspective: "It sounds funny, but I've played 21, 22 years. I'm 45, and I've come upon 300 wins, and I'm thinking, *I only have 211 more to catch Cy Young.*"

Bruce Bochy

Bruce Bochy had already achieved managerial excellence by the time he took over the Giants' post prior to the 2007 season. The former major league catcher had managed the San Diego Padres for 12 seasons before signing a four-year contract with the Giants to succeed Felipe Alou on October 27, 2006.

Bochy was born in Landes de Bussac, France, where his father was a U.S. Army officer, but he grew up in Virginia before moving to Melbourne, Florida, where he attended Melbourne High School. After graduating, he attended Brevard Community College before transferring to Florida State University. A strapping catcher with good size and a powerful bat, Bochy was drafted by the Houston Astros in the first round of the 1975 major league draft (24th overall).

He reached the major leagues three years later, becoming one of eight major leaguers to be born in France. He had two hits in his debut game against Mets right-hander Craig Swann. But he could not win the starting job, and when Alan Ashby took over as the backup, the Astros traded him to the Mets, who sent him back to the minor leagues at Tidewater, their Triple A affiliate.

Bochy has a large head—literally—which caused some problems once the Mets called him to the major leagues in 1982. The club's equipment manager could not find a helmet large enough to fit him, which prevented him from playing until the helmet he wore with Tidewater arrived.

Bochy went to the San Diego Padres in 1983, where he served as Terry Kennedy's backup. While with the Padres, they won their first National League pennant in 1984 before meeting—and losing to—the Detroit Tigers in the World Series; he played in one game during the Series. As a historic footnote, Bochy caught Padres right-hander Eric Show on September 11, 1985, which was the night the Padres played the Cincinnati Reds and Pete Rose broke Ty Cobb's career hits mark with a hit off Show.

The Padres had a pair of talented catchers pushing up from the minor leagues, so after the 1987 season, he retired, clearing the way for the arrival of Mark Parent and Benito Santiago. Bochy hit .239 with 26 home runs in 802 career at-bats. While the experience of not playing did not allow Bochy to improve his skills, it did allow him to learn the game by watching from the bench. He became a minor league manager in the Padres organization, which led to him becoming the third-base coach for the major league club in 1993.

The Padres finished in last place in the National League West in 1994, which prompted the firing of manager Jim Riggleman. Bochy was promoted to take his place, making him the first former Padres player to manage the team. In 1996 the Padres compiled the best record in the National League West, and Bochy came away with National League Manager of the Year honors. Then in 1998 the Padres won 98 games en route to their second-ever appearance in the Fall Classic, where they were swept by the New York Yankees.

By the time his tenure as the Padres manager had run its course, he had led the team to four postseason appearances, claiming division titles in 1996, 1998, 2005, and 2006. He won more than 900 games as the Padres manager, which was quite an accomplishment based on the fact that at times the Padres fielded "cost-effective" teams.

In addition to having one of the largest cap sizes in Major League Baseball at 8¾, he also has another oddity among his features. The eyelashes over Boche's right eye have a blonde hue as a result of a chemical reaction he incurred while working at a furniture-refinishing shop as a youngster.

Foreign-Born Major League Managers

Bruce Bochy, who was born in France, is part of a unique club as one of the few managers in major league history to be born on foreign soil. Here is a look at the list of major league managers who were born outside the United States by country of birth:

Australia
Joe Quinn

Canada
George Gibson
Arthur Irwin
Fred Lake
Bill Watkins

Cuba
Preston Gomez
Fredi Gonzalez
Mike Gonzalez
Marty Martinez
Cookie Rojas
Tony Perez
Carlos Tosca

Dominican Republic
Manny Acta
Felipe Alou
Tony Pena
Luis Pujols

England
Tom Brown
Dick Higham
Al Reach

Harry Smith
Harry Wright

France
Bruce Bochy

Germany
Ron Gardenhire
Joe Miller
Chris Von der Ahe

Ireland
Tommy Bond
Patsy Donovan
Jack Doyle
Fergy Malone
Mike Scanlon
Ted Sullivan

Scotland
Jim McCormick
Hugh Nicol

Venezuela
Ozzie Guillen
Al Pedrique

Wales
Jimmy Austin

Sources

Alexander, Charles. *John McGraw* (Lincoln, NE: University of Nebraska Press, 1995).

Allen, Bob, and Bill Gilbert. *The 500 Home Run Club: Baseball's 16 Greatest Home Run Hitters from Babe Ruth to Mark McGwire* (Champaign, IL: Sports Publishing LLC, 2000).

Barra, Allen. *Brushbacks and Knockdowns: The Greatest Baseball Debates of Two Centuries* (New York: Macmillan Publishers, 2004).

Doxsie, Don. *Iron Man McGinnity: A Baseball Biography* (Jefferson, NC: McFarland and Company, 2009).

James, Bill. *The New Bill James Historical Baseball Abstract* (New York: Free Press, 2003).

Kalb, Elliott. *Who's Better, Who's Best in Baseball? Mr. Stats Sets the Record Straight on the Top 75 Players of All-Time* (New York: McGraw-Hill, 2005).

Leventhal, Josh, and Jessica Macmurray. *Take Me Out to the Ballpark: An Illustrated Tour of Baseball Parks Past and Present* (rev. ed.) (New York: Black Dog and Leventhal Publishers, 2006).

Linge, Mary Kay. *Willie Mays: A Biography* (Westport, CT: Greenwood Press, 2005).

Lombardi, Stephen M. *The Baseball Same Game: Finding Comparable Players from the National Pastime* (Lincoln, NE: iUniverse, 2005).

Walsh, Joan, C.W. Nevius, Larry Baer, and Peter Magowan. *Splash Hit! PacBell Park and the San Francisco Giants* (San Francisco: Chronicle Books, 2001).

Publications and Websites

2010 Giants Media Guide
Atlanta Journal Constitution
Baseball Digest
Chicago Tribune
ESPN.com

MLB.com
New York Times
Sports Illustrated
Time magazine